The Devil Loves a Shining Mark

The Devil Loves a Shining Mark

The Story of My Life
Jim Vaus
with Julie Maxey

Word Books, Publisher
Waco, Texas

The Devil Loves a Shining Mark

Scripture quotations from The Living Bible, copyright
© Tyndale House, 1971.

Library of Congress catalog card number: 73-91555

To my wife,
who makes
our happy times
sweeter,
and sees the joy
hidden in the sad.

Foreword

I've known Jim Vaus since he worked for me in the syndicate. I stuck it out in the rackets and ended up serving two long jail terms. Jim, who'd already served two short ones, took a look where he was headed working for me, and changed his life.

When he came back from Billy Graham's tent meeting and told me he'd converted to Christianity, I didn't know what he was saying. I'm a Jew and thought gentiles were already Christians. He explained you've got to give your life to Christ to be a real Christian. I thought it was a beautiful thing. I told him, "I hope your heart and soul are in this thing. I hope you aren't just taking a flier. Never turn back."

That was in 1949. Jim's life since then speaks for itself. He's a man who shows he cares about others. He had the guts to quit the syndicate and move on to do good by kids who needed him. I admire and love the guy. He never turned back. He's still helping troubled kids. And he never turned his back on me. Now I think I know just about as much about Christianity as Jim. And every time Billy Graham wrote a book, he would send me a copy in the pen.

When I came home from jail this last time, Jim was ready with help. He's still my friend.

MICKEY COHEN
Los Angeles, California

Introduction

One night at a tent meeting in Los Angeles my associates told me a gangster who worked for syndicate boss Mickey Cohen was in the audience. "We don't know why. Maybe he's just curious," they said. But they were trembling.

An usher asked this man to come forward when I gave the invitation. He was hostile and gruffly refused. Then, a few minutes later, because of a reason no one fully understood, Jim Vaus decided to come forward, to give his life to Christ. People thought it was a big hoax, a fraud. It would never last, they said, he was too bad to change. But I talked to him personally that night and believed he was sincere. At the time, Jim thought he might "get it" from syndicate members because he was quitting.

That was in 1949 and he did quit to become one of the great Christian leaders. In New York he contributed his time and love working in Harlem. Now on the west coast he continues to live the life he promised the Lord he would twenty-five years ago.

BILLY GRAHAM
Montreat, North Carolina

1 Chapter

"The only mistake the White House made about Watergate is they didn't get you to do the tapping. They got a bunch of amateurs, boys to do a man's job. They should have got you to do the work. The country wouldn't have gotten into this mess." Mickey Cohen called to tell me that.

As I hung up the phone I was struck by the difference in my life today from the 1940s, when I worked as a wiretapper for Cohen during his reign as Godfather of southern California.

My eyes skimmed across the plaid sofa in my office and returned to the beige phone. I wondered, is Cohen right? If the White House had asked me to do the tapping, would the nation have ever heard the word "Watergate"? That caper is only a drop in the sea of routine political spying—a tradition I was part of in Los Angeles twenty-five years ago. And I never got caught.

Imagine, being captured in the opponent's territory, equipment dangling. The art of tapping is sophisticated far beyond the Watergate boys' break-in approach. They didn't even need to get near the target building. An unseen laser beam can turn a windowpane into a microphone. Sound waves then boomerang off the window back onto the beam to a listening post a block or more away.

During my wiretapping days I shared some of my know-how with Samuel Dash. At that time he was on the district attorney's staff in Philadelphia, doing a state-by-state study of wiretapping for the Pennsylvania Bar Association. He wanted to know about the uses of wiretapping in law enforcement, private industry, and crime, all of which I'd done. The report grew into his classic book, *The Eavesdroppers*. It was Samuel Dash who would later be chosen chief counsel for the Watergate Committee.

As Mickey Cohen says, "When you like doing something, you do it well." He did, and so did I. He lured me into the racketeer underworld where he bossed a brisk bookmaking business on his way up to the powerful peak of syndicate king. That top spot wasn't easy to win. It was tougher to keep.

Cohen, a New York boy, busied himself slugging his way up. "I got a kick out of it," he says. Indeed! He got kicks, punches, bullets, and other fringe benefits from his syndicate association. Alliances shifted faster than square-dance partners. To keep up, he kept moving. Then came a death in the family.

Bugsey Segal, the reigning top banana, was shot dead in Virginia Hill's home. The rumbles began even before his body could be shipped to the L.A. morgue. The uneasy truce that family members Mickey Cohen and Jack Dragna had established, never more stable than a paper kite in a hurricane, ripped apart. The

12

fragments of the organization began circling the rich southern California racketlands like vultures after prey. The squabble that started over who got control swelled into a deadly serious war, centering in Hollywood's Sunset Strip. Local lawmen and the FBI were aware of the infighting. It was impossible not to be. They kept their hands off, hoping the mobsters would erase each other from the scene. The war dragged on, got grittier, and gained a name, the Battle of Sunset Strip.

The gangs used up three years settling the question of who would run the rackets. No one knows the body count, though every side lost many lives. Mickey Cohen wanted to be sure he kept himself in one piece.

It was no easy trick for Cohen to keep his head out of the way of a rival's shot. And, though no one bothered the boys at war, he had the added worry of the police busting him for bookmaking. That's why he eventually came to me.

I was hazy about who Mickey Cohen was when one of his henchmen first approached me. I didn't have a hint of his power, although I'd heard his name and seen it in the papers under the slug, "Czar of Sunset Strip." I thought he wanted the usual check on his wife, maybe a friend. I agreed to meet Cohen at his haberdashery on the Strip. What did I have to lose?

It was a shop that Hollywood set designers couldn't have improved upon. The prices Cohen charged for shirts and ties, I paid for jackets. Most of the clothes were stored in vaultlike closets behind sliding doors that matched the polished walnut walls. The salesman was dressed for a Cadillac ad. His fishy look let me know he wondered, as much as I began to, why I was there. I announced myself while trying to smooth the wrinkles from my pants. The salesman relayed my message and my presence to the inner office. The return message: Cohen was being measured for a suit. Please wait.

13

That wait turned into forty-five minutes. Just when I thought I had stared at an outrageously priced tie long enough, I was summoned. I walked through a steel-plated door into Cohen's inner quarters. It became obvious that Cohen's business was more than selling clothes. It was also clear that no one got into his sanctuary without an invitation.

Mickey Cohen, immaculate, more perfectly dressed than the salesman, sat behind a circular desk, his back facing the wall. No one spoke.

I offered, hesitantly, "I'm Jim Vaus."

My voice sounded like thunder breaking into a silent summer day. "Vaus," said Cohen, never taking his brown eyes off me, "I've heard the police planted a mike in my house. Did you do it?"

"Not me," said my voice. I was considerably calmer now that I knew what he wanted. I was innocent. "I don't even know where you live."

Cohen continued, "If my house is bugged, can you find out where it is and get it out for me?"

"Mr. Cohen, I only install them. I don't take them out," I replied. I thought that would end the conversation.

He gave me a long sizing up, his face expressionless. His right hand reached into his pocket like a fisherman's into a bait tank, and pulled out a fat roll of crackling new one-hundred-dollar bills. He peeled off three or four like they were artichoke leaves.

"Vaus," he murmured, "what business did you say you were in?"

"Uh, I think it's about to expand."

On my way to Cohen's house in Westwood, escorted by his lieutenant Neddie Herbert, I started having some doubts about this job. They grew. These weren't ordinary customers I was dealing with. What would happen if I didn't come through for them? I tried to blot the headlines that loomed up in my thoughts, the ones detailing the wretched acts the syndicate supposedly performed on people out of favor.

Neddie led me into the spacious blue and white house. He played an elaborate game, so no one listening would be wise to our search. Taking giant tiptoe steps, Neddie played the clown, with finger to mouth from chin to nose, to signify silence. We played follow the leader around the whole house. I was most impressed with Cohen's wall-to-wall closet filled with suits, shoes, and shirts stacked to the ceiling. I didn't know one person could have so many clothes. And he had me wait while he was fitted for more.

Herbert and I went out the back door into the yard. I did a little digging and unearthed a gem. It was a rubber-covered lead cable, typical of most telephone wires, only this wire was planted in the ground with surgical precision. I knew we were on to something.

To track down the bug we disconnected all the electrical appliances, even the gas stove's electric clock. The electric meter still registered drift, or electric current flow. I unscrewed each fuse in the box, one by one, to match the one controlling the drift to the area of the house the fuse served. I had to go through all of them before I found the right one. I trailed the electric flow to the fireplace by using a device I'd made. The outside cable, I reasoned, was run under the house to connect with the bug in the fireplace. I couldn't very well rip up the floor, so I cut a hole inside the wood storage area, where no one would notice any later patching. A jockey might have slipped through the hole easily, but I had to get my six-foot-four inch frame and three hundred pounds through it. I wriggled down, finally disappearing beneath the floor while Neddie watched in amazement. I'm sure his private bet was that there was no way I would make it.

I turned my flashlight on. Bingo. I spied the small line amplifier and mike three feet away. Whoever put it in had taken pains. This was a sophisticated installation. I stifled my victory yell and told Neddie I had it.

"Don't move," he ordered. Then he phoned the boss. "Cohen is on his way. He wants to see everything," Neddie said.

That underground cave was not exactly where I wanted to be. I didn't have any space to stretch. But I spent the next hour and a half there until Cohen arrived. I disconnected the wires so the ears on the end of the line knew they'd been cut off. Cohen was ecstatic. By the time he got there I didn't care anymore if he was happy or not, I just wanted to be released from that form-fitting cellar. It took a quarter of an hour to dislodge myself.

After the ordeal we met in his room. He held out some more one-hundred-dollar bills as a bonus, then offered me another job. The work was setting up electronic devices to protect Cohen. He was the only one during that period of my life who never wanted me to tap a wire for him.

The day after I nipped the bug in Cohen's home, I saw the reach of his power. He had a complete copy of the top secret log of conversations the police had taped at his house. I began paying more attention.

"My connection in the police department gave me the log," *Cohen remembers. "The police couldn't figure out how I got it. I had the combination: power to make people respect me, the money to pay them off, and people feared me. I had the strength of making someone do what I wanted him to do. I controlled the sheriff's office, the district attorney's office, and the politics of the time."*

2 Chapter

My wiretapping career began innocently enough, and on the right side of the law. I had volunteered to manage an apartment house for a short time to help out a friend. One of the girls in the apartment house decided to work at home entertaining men in her room for money. Tenants complained to me and I in turn complained to the police. A trio of young detectives answered my call. I told them about Marge's activities.

"Is anyone with her now?" one asked.

"Yes, if he hasn't left," I replied. "I just saw her leading a stranger down the hall."

The three took off toward Marge's apartment. As they approached the door they heard voices, but the noise was too muffled to understand. I horned in on the case and led the men around to the outside window. We didn't have any better luck there. The detectives were convinced she was working as a prostitute, yet Marge was still free to continue. No proof, no prosecution.

"Don't you have a device that can listen behind closed doors?" I asked.

I was surprised when they answered, "We sure don't." They looked at me as if I were a strange bird for asking such a question. It probably did sound odd coming from an apartment house manager. There's no way they could have known that I was just pinch-hitting for a friend and that electronics was my business. Electronics fascinated me. I loved it! My firm, Electronic Engineering Consultants, was growing as the public gradually discovered electronics. We installed custom radio and intercom systems. We wired gates and garages so they'd open electronically. It's all routine stuff today, like wiretapping, but it wasn't in the forties.

I grabbed the challenge of solving a new electronics problem and offered to design some special equipment so they could eavesdrop on Marge. All we'd need was a concealed microphone connected to a wire recorder. When I described what I was going to make, the detectives acted like I was speaking in tongues. They thought the idea was terrific, but they were skeptical about its being carried out. Not skeptical enough, however, to keep them from coming back the next night. That gave me about twenty-four hours to craft a crude wiretap device. I used most of those hours to design and refine the bugs. I hid the mike in a vase in Marge's room while she was out marketing.

The next night Marge and the unlucky friend of the moment talked themselves right into the open arms of the detectives. Marge was arrested for violating City Ordinance MC 4107.

I had enjoyed meeting the challenge. The tenants were happy, and so were the police. They acted like kids with a new Christmas toy.

My police buddies were back knocking at my door in less than a week. I got a pep talk about what a great

job I'd done, then I got a request for a repeat performance. I obliged, and tried to be on call whenever a
wiretapping job came up. The aura of working with
them was like a fox hunt. I liked being in on the chase
to catch a criminal, and it was obvious they needed my
help.

The police had more than enough to keep them
busy in the heyday of Hollywood. One woman cashing
in on this loose living was Brenda Allen. The newspapers described her as the "Hollywood Vice Queen."
This smart madam didn't keep house. She ran her call
girls strictly by phone working through a switchboard.
Brenda would call in, never leaving her own phone
number. She got her picture listed in the players' direc-
tory, a catalog of actors, and bribed taxi drivers to hand
out business cards. It was a successful ad campaign;
Brenda's clients were famous faces of the forties.

The officer in charge of the vice division, Lieutenant
Blair, was a tough cop who wanted her out of business.
The rumor around town was that Brenda paid off the
vice squad. Blair didn't think she did much for the
department's reputation.

"She doesn't pay me off, and I'm out to get her,"
Blair raged to me.

"What's stopping you?" I asked.

"Brenda's no dummy," he said. "She runs her business by phone, sends her girls to meet men at different
spots, never the same, never her home. We don't even
have her phone number or an inkling of where she
lives."

What Blair needed was a device that could listen in
on a telephone chat while the parties remained oblivi-
ous to the fact that they had an audience. I thought that
was possible. The kicker was that he wanted to be able
to determine what phone number had been dialed. He
was thinking ahead to other uses for this gadget, like

breaking up the bookmaking rackets. It took weeks of off-hours experimenting to put together the impulse indicator that determined the number dialed and the device that made it possible to bug a conversation without contacting the line.

Just as I finished the device, we got a lucky break—an address for Brenda. I tapped into her line so the police could hear her scheduling appointments. We traced the number Brenda dialed and then followed her. She went to keep her appointment. So did the police. They dogged Brenda's trail until she got caught and was convicted of pandering. The case broke open in banner headlines, some about me and the wire recordings I'd made. Officials were fascinated; so much so I was jailed for twenty-four hours before I half convinced someone that I had truly destroyed the recordings, which I had. I'm not sure anyone ever believed I did.

Police work fed my ego, not my wallet. The only money I pocketed was for equipment the department continued to use. That was rare. So were the occasional twenty-five-dollar bonuses. While my extracurricular jobs for the police were in many ways worthwhile, they were a financial disaster. I helped ease my bills by ordering electronic equipment on forged purchase orders. I usually chose major movie studios for victims. Sometimes I'd have the equipment delivered at a phony address. I'd pick up the equipment, but not the bill. I saved a lot of money this way and the police never knew they were solving crimes with stolen equipment.

Wiretapping for the police, especially with all the publicity that built up around the Brenda Allen case, led to my working for Barney Ruditsky, a retired New York cop who was doing private detective work. Barney worked for a parade of famous, and not so famous, people around Sunset Strip who nurtured real or imagined fears about the activities of their spouses, friends, or enemies. I was ready for some new business when he called.

When I arrived in Barney's office, I found the young star Mickey Rooney and his manager. Rooney's manager was holding a fan made of five one-hundred-dollar bills.

"It's for you, Vaus," said Rooney, "if you can tap into the phone number on this piece of paper. You've got five minutes."

I would have done almost anything in the next five minutes for that money. Imagine an old-time movie of a man running triple time with a honky-tonk piano playing in the background and you'll know how fast I raced out to my car, grabbed the equipment, ran back in, and set up.

I dialed the number and was lucky enough to plug into a conversation. We all drew into a semicircle around the phone and listened to a male voice betting on the horses.

"That's my houseboy. He's always tossing money away on the ponies. Just can't hit a winner," chuckled Rooney.

But Rooney wasn't there to listen to his houseboy. Five minutes later he got what he wanted. His wife picked up the phone and began talking intimately to a man. This got Rooney and his lawyer the evidence they needed to prove adultery for his upcoming divorce, and me $500 for fifteen minutes work.

I knew a gold mine when I saw it and I panned for nuggets. The harness that checked many a divorce in Hollywood, and the rest of California, was the law that forced property to be equally divided unless one spouse could prove the other had committed adultery. I got lots of jobs. Rooney sent me to help Errol Flynn, whose wife was running around with Dick Haymes. Dick Haymes's

21

wife was with John Ireland. It was a game of musical beds that made *Peyton Place* seem tame. I made a good living from these stars and other Hollywood notables like bandleader Xavier Cugat.

Tapping had to pay. If the instigator of the tap didn't want to shell out, I'd threaten to turn over the tapes to the victim. However, there were moments when I nearly ended up like the Watergate boys, caught. I set out to plant a mike at actress Joanne Drew's house when everyone was out. I was flat on my back beneath the house when I heard footsteps above. I stayed hidden until things settled down up there and, casually as I could, crawled out. A neighbor was watching, so I picked up my tool case, waved to him and left. No one questioned me. If I looked confident, I discovered that no one bothered to ask me who I was. People wait until they see a so-called suspicious type, which most criminals aren't.

My business expanded. Private companies checked on their competitors. Politicians were just as interested as they are now in what others were up to. I once had a wire recording between two California politicians that a Washington newspaper knew would be a hot story. It must have been good, because an ambassador from the paper flew to California to offer me $10,000 for the recordings. But that was later in my career. I refused.

In those days, when morality was the last thing on my mind and money the first, I had an easy time spying on peoples' private lives with no thought as to the consequences.

I did personal tapping for J. Paul Getty, but my biggest undertaking was protecting his Malibu estate. He feared something, perhaps kidnapers, and wanted the place secure against all intruders. I surrounded his estate with what newspaper stories miscalled radar. It was actually infrared light that set off an alarm when its rays were interrupted. I installed an electric gate that would close instantly. Getty himself drove his car back and forth while I adjusted the timing of the gate. It seemed a funny way for one of the richest men in the world to spend his afternoon. I added another layer of infrared light around the house. Still a third electronic block banded Getty's bedroom. As far as I know, no one ever tried to get through those three tiers of electronic protection. I don't think anyone on the ground could have.

When I first went to work for Cohen I thought I could keep up with my police jobs. Cohen didn't mind, but it got rather cozy. I knew too much to serve two masters. It was a severe case of conflict of interest.

Would I work for the law or a gangster? It was a simple decision. Mickey Cohen offered more money, and he paid wages in cash. No need to tell the Internal Revenue Service.

His operations were centered around bookmaking. It's strange now to see off track betting booths, tidy and legal, where anyone can place a bet. During my days with Cohen, betting off track was a crime, though placing a bet on a horse at the track was legitimate. Cohen was just ahead of the trend. Although not an educated man, Cohen was a genius at keeping numbers of bets, wins, races, and losses in his head. He didn't want evidence on paper that could be used against him. The police kept a constant eye on Cohen's activities. There's nothing they'd have liked better than to lock him up. But he was too cagey for that and, besides, his employees were loyal. When the Los Angeles County Grand Jury attempted to investigate underworld associations, the tables were turned on the police. I was one of those who falsely testified against an innocent police sergeant, Sergeant E.V. Jackson, to protect the syndicate. We twisted the evidence to make it appear that Jackson was a part of Brenda Allen's operation. Jackson was evicted from the department and the investigation dropped.

My most important job was to protect Cohen during the Battle of Sunset Strip. I moved my electronics company into the basement of Cohen's haberdashery. It worked out fine but I always did feel underdressed when I had to meet with Cohen in the upstairs shop.

He kept his profile low during those years of war, fearing his head would be shot off. Cohen's car was better equipped than an armored tank. It had shatterproof glass and more gimmicks than a good cook's kitchen. The hidden compartments were the best. Some hid guns or "pieces." It was a standing joke that although the police had given the car a thorough search, they still couldn't come up with the equipment. If all those elaborate devices seem dramatic, they were. So were the attempts on Cohen's life.

The fancy car wasn't foolproof. To add another dimension of security, I worked out an electrical signal board for his Sunset Strip office. With this board, Cohen could tell his escorts the route he was going to drive home.

I ran periodic checks on his home for bugs and phone taps. I strung a ring of infrared light, the same I'd used on Getty's estate, around Cohen's place. I electrified the garage door so Cohen could open it from the car and wouldn't have to expose himself. (These devices are common today, but were almost unheard of then.) I added one other touch, a car control switch on the lights throughout his property. One dark night when Cohen lit the lights on his way into the garage, bullets from both sides of the driveway pelted his car. The windshield disappeared, so did Cohen. He dropped to the floor, gunned the engine, and drove the car blind to Wilshire Boulevard where he did a jack-in-the-box

24

pop-up. The second time he headed home that night he fortified himself with Neddie Herbert and heavy equipment, but the snipers had vanished.

I had my own scare. While relaxing one evening at Cohen's house the alarm screamed, indicating the infrared fence had been crossed. I sprang out of my easy chair toward the door and scrambled over people into the yard. I caught sight of a flicker like a firefly sprinting across the grass. This firefly was a lighted fuse. I grabbed it. A six-inch TNT bomb rolled out of a hiding place under the house. I quickly pulled out the fuse and just stood there looking at that bomb for a long time.

Violence stormed all around me. Men I knew were likely to die at any moment. Hooky Rothman, a soldier of Cohen's, fell one day in my office. A quirk of Cohen's saved his own skin on that particular occasion. He always had a thing about being clean. His morning bath lasted for hours. Toothbrushing took half an hour and a tube of toothpaste. He constantly washed his hands. And, with all those suits in his closet, he never wore one more than a couple of times. Shoes stayed on his feet only as long as they looked like they were fresh out of the box. Even today, he picks up four tissues to hold a telephone receiver.

The day Hooky got it, Cohen was on his way into my office. He didn't bother to greet me or the three or four others standing around, but headed straight to the john to wash up. Gunmen cruised in on his heels shooting, then took off. Buckshot burst like fireworks and caught Hooky. He had been standing near the front and didn't have a chance to duck. That was the first time I'd seen anyone shot and killed. The incident jarred me enough so that I reflected about life, death, and God, but that was only a momentary reflection. Then I rushed right back into Cohen's world.

Neddie Herbert was next. Another mistake. He got

the bullet aimed at Cohen in a shoot-out at Sherry's Restaurant on the Strip. A few of these happenings, and Cohen adopted the habit of traveling with a group of heavies for bodyguards. Cohen's body is tough from boxing as a youth but he is not very tall. The press dubbed his entourage, "Snow White and the Seven Dwarfs."

Cohen's life wasn't always punctuated by shots. There were quiet times, and party times. I was privileged to share Cohen's hospitality and spent a lot of time at the house. There were always ten or twelve for dinner, even if Cohen wasn't at home. To Cohen, pretty-faced, sexy starlets meant nothing more than a staple a good host could offer. He wasn't interested himself. He was married to La Vonne, his wife of eighteen years, and that was where his attention stayed. But at his salon, the wine and women were hand-picked like perfect fruit and available to his guests. Famous stars like George Raft and Red Skelton also appeared, as well as noted businessmen and lawyers. Those evenings were social for the most part. If Cohen wanted to talk to someone about business, he'd call him over to a corner huddle. I enjoyed being in the same room, if not in the same circle, with these well-known people.

Another famous friend of Cohen's was Frank Sinatra. One evening as Cohen drove down Sunset Boulevard, Sinatra, seeing who it was, hailed the car. Cohen saw him, but there are times when you have to pass up a friend. His sixth sense was at work and he drove right by the startled Sinatra. Cohen smelled trouble up the road and didn't want Sinatra to get hurt. He was right. A few miles further on, a rival's machine gun let loose into the passenger side of the car.

Night club life was not only dangerous for Cohen; on a lighter side, it got to be expensive. Cohen remembers, *"In those days I wouldn't keep any money in my pocket that* *wasn't new and clean. I've got a phobia about my clothing. My bookkeeper saw that I never ran short of pocket money. He got me my new money, something like $800–$1500 each day, so my pockets and hands wouldn't get dirty. I became a sitting duck for waiters. The word got around, and I'd get back the grimiest looking bills in the restaurant. I wouldn't touch it, and told the waiters to keep the change.*"

Outside the syndicate life I lived another identity, that of husband and father. Though my actions at that time weren't worthy of her, life with Alice has always been a joy. (We'll soon celebrate our twenty-seventh wedding anniversary.) She is a happy person who doesn't entertain herself by nagging or picking on people. She didn't back then either. Our interests were ourselves, our one-year-old child Madeline, and our home. We bought a ranch house nestled in a walnut grove in Baldwin Park, a suburb of Los Angeles. It was almost all farm land back in the forties.

Alice likes interior decorating and added touches to our home no one else would have thought of. It was a comfortable place I enjoyed. We attended South Hollywood Presbyterian Church on Sundays. I went mainly to escort Alice, but although I worked for Cohen, church wasn't totally alien to my character. I'd sit and listen to the sermon, but my attention span was short. I thought, when the time was right, when I was rich enough, when I was ready, I'd make a commitment. When I got busier and more deeply rooted in the racket work, my church-going slowed down. I had only a little time for Alice, and less for God.

Alice realized something was sour, but she had no reason to ask about what I was doing or which side of the law I was on.

3

Chapter

I have almost made a career out of not being what people think I am, for evil *and* for good.

My parents expected me to keep up the family tradition. Dad was an ordained Baptist preacher who taught Old Testament subjects at the Bible Institute of Los Angeles, which later became Biola College. Church had been part of the Vaus's life since the 1800s when Scotsman Samuel Vaus founded the Pennypacker Church, the first Baptist church in Pennsylvania. My parents' agenda said that I would finish college, then follow my father's footsteps into the ministry, as he had followed others before him. It would take thirty years for me to carry out their wishes, and the life I led in the interim was as different from the one they'd imagined, as a watermelon growing on a grapevine.

They had every reason to expect me to be a "good" boy. I'd been raised in a Christian family. My parents loved my sisters and me, but they exercised rigid controls. They held the reins tight. We weren't allowed to go to dances or movies, both of which I would have loved. They thought we should be kept away from questionable entertainment and taught morality.

But morality can't be smeared on like butter on bread. It just didn't seep through, though as a youth I acted the part they wanted to see played. I studied my Bible and I was there for family prayer with my sisters, Virginia and Betty. I learned to sit and listen during our get-togethers, or at least appear to listen. The thought, "I don't want to go," never occurred to me. When I got bored, my mind coasted on fantasies overflowing with wanderlust. I wasn't touched, though I replayed the flowery phrases, projected the good Christian facade, and blended into the church structures. I went to the Church of the Open Door, a Protestant nondenominational church on Hope Street in Los Angeles. I plunged into the social swim and was elected president of the junior high-school group, then the high-school youth chapter. That's where most of my friends were. That's why I went. When Mother was worried that I was hooked on the social activities and not Christ's message, she told me, "The devil loves a shining mark." But I paid no heed.

I did strike up an alliance with an adult named Atwood Chambers, an L.A. streetcar conductor who rented a room in our house. He sparked an interest in electronics that's continued all my life. Chambers was a quiet man who spent his leisure hours tinkering in electronics. Like a bird building a nest, he bought wires and parts and put them together to make fascinating inventions. He was meticulous, working on a radio with the care of a watchmaker. I was allowed to watch and became a self-styled apprentice, treasuring the parts Chambers threw away. I started drilling holes and stringing wires like garlands all over the house. I soon inherited the loft above our garage, probably because my mother couldn't stand one more buzzer system decking her halls. In my workshop retreat I experimented, building my own radios just like Atwood Chambers, then went on to do my own exploring of the wonders of electronics.

After a lot of trial and error, I managed to string together components and wires that grew into a broadcast system for church. I went along with them as the announcer. In high school I made sure I attended all the math and science courses that would help me in electronics. Electronics work was all play, it was so easy for me. No one could have predicted then, when I was fifteen and inventing electronic gadgets in my loft, that I'd be working for Mickey Cohen. But, then, I don't think anyone could have predicted that before I ever got near Cohen, I'd be thrown out of college and then into jail for armed robbery.

Like kids do, I let life happen to me. I went to Biola College where my father taught. I can't give a good answer why, except to please my father. I felt boxed in and restless. My parents and I agreed it was time for me to try a campus away from home. In 1937 I took the train to Wheaton, a Christian college in Illinois. I'd never been out of southern California and my eyes remained fixed on the window, watching the shifting scenery as we crossed the country. I can still see the mountains growing big as the train roared toward them, fading as we left them behind, speeding on over the flatlands of the midwest. I've made the trip many times since, but it has never again been so heady. It was my first time on my own.

At Wheaton my counselor claimed I wasn't making the most of my potential, and urged me to knuckle down. It was a pleasant, bland year and so were my grades—about a C average. I wasn't expelled from Wheaton, but the college was lukewarm about my casual attitude, and after a summer back home in California I trekked back to the Bible Institute.

That year I built my reputation for being high-spirited when I performed my first wiretap escapade.

Revenge, not curiosity, was my motive. I was furious at a girl, Annie, for an offhanded crack she'd made about me, and was ready to even the score. The following afternoon I fast-talked the elevator operator into running me up to the girls' territory, the top floor. I got him to keep watch for ten minutes, the time it took me to plant my microphone in Annie's room. I buried a loudspeaker beneath her bed and slipped the wires out the window. Then I tiptoed back to the elevator, undetected. I connected the wires from Annie's window to my equipment and went down to dinner. After I had eaten, I excused myself and went straight to my room to wait.

A half-hour dragged by before I heard Annie and a girlfriend enter her room, giggling. The evening's topic, which they went into in great detail, was which boys they liked and why. I recorded their debate. At "lights out" I flipped the switch. "Good evening, this is Fu Man Chu," I boomed. I quickly switched back to hear the reaction. Screams. Silence. Then a flock of twittery voices. "I tell you he's under the bed," Annie wailed. When all the flutter stopped, I flipped over to talk. We chatted back and forth, being witty. She thought it was a terrific prank until I told her I'd taped her earlier chatter. Annie didn't believe me so I played her a portion. She was both mad and embarrassed. I loved it. However, when the word got out, neither my father nor the dean of women was as amused as I was.

I became a busy man on campus and zeroed in on my pet project, the *Biolan,* our yearbook. Traditionally, advertisements were sold to cover the cost of publishing the book. I devised another way to rake in some cash: a show for the public. The show looked like it was a smash. I put a lot of time into that program, which was a dandy. Three thousand people came. As the crowd circulated I quickly calculated a return of several hundred dollars. A conservative estimate.

I didn't have proof enough to cry "Thief!" but a bundle of our earnings got stashed in someone else's piggy bank. The *Biolan* fund netted under one hundred dollars. I was tooth-grinding mad about being taken. In my fury I abandoned reason and took off with the money we'd made from ads and the pittance gathered from the show. I bought a plane ticket with the stolen funds and flew to Florida, a state I had always wanted to see. I was still sizzling when I got on the plane but by the time the wheels touched the ground, my anger had cooled and, too late, I felt isolated and foolish.

Florida was like a picture postcard—beautiful, but two-dimensional. I was miserable. There was no one to talk to and nothing to do so I finally collected myself and called my family. Dad wired money.

The train ride home was ghastly. I didn't see a thing out the window. I was focused on my immediate future, the embarrassment of facing my parents, friends, and worse, the reaction at school.

My mother and father suffered from a mild case of shock. They didn't shun me, but clearly, they were stunned by my behavior. Dad arranged for me to borrow money from a friend of the family and pay back the school. I did, and was promptly expelled.

Then, when I could have used friends, my ties were severed. First the school, then the church, said, "Don't come back." The loss of my church friends was the greatest. I wonder if my life would have taken the twists it did if the church had been supportive. Maybe they were scared my actions would spread like a disease.

I turned my part-time college job into a full-time

occupation. I wrapped packages at the Broadway Department Store, a good way to earn extra dollars but hardly a stimulating way to spend a day. Out of my fifty-cents-an-hour wages, I had to pay back my loan and contribute to my keep at home. At this rate, even working overtime occasionally, my wallet didn't fatten rapidly. That made me short on two things: friends and cash.

I got to know some of the guys working as wrappers and delivery boys. They weren't great buddies but they were fun to joke around with. When one of them, Schwartz, hit me for a twenty-dollar loan I was eager as a puppy to help. I wanted to come through with something for someone to puff up my flattened ego. It didn't matter how. The problem was, I didn't have the money and there was no way my family would lend me any. My paycheck wasn't due for a week. I'll never understand exactly how I arrived at it, but I found another answer. I'd go get it.

I opened the squeaky drawer hiding Dad's old .32 Harrison-Richards revolver. It hadn't been fired in years but I wasn't going to shoot anyone anyway. I needed a prop. I put on my jacket, put the gun under it, and asked Dad for the car.

I drove to plush Beverly Hills. Cruising down a tree-lined side street I became Robin Hood, helping a poor friend. I spotted a lone man. I parked the car and followed him on foot.

"This is a holdup," I said when I reached him. "Give me your wallet." I showed him the gun and he handed over his wallet. I told him to walk on and not look back, as a robber is supposed to do. He called back pleading for his driver's license. That's not what I was after so I went back and handed it to him.

I didn't find out until the next day, when I answered the page on the store intercom and reported to a room

34

full of police, that my Broadway employee's I.D. card had slipped out of my jacket pocket at the scene of the crime.

My parents arrived, dragging along my mother's brother to help because he had been in the L.A. political scene. There wasn't a thing they or he could do to unwind me from the tangle. I had already signed a confession of armed robbery.

When I should have looked to God for help, I looked away. I was sorry I'd been caught. Who wouldn't be? But I didn't feel it so strongly that it changed any of my thinking. I was locked in an amoral pose as if frozen inside an ice cube. I may have told my parents that I repented, but if so, it was to win approval, not because I was sincere. My only feeling after I had taken the guy's wallet was that I'd done a pretty fair job. If I hadn't been caught, I might have tried it again—especially since all I got in my first and only role as an armed robber was fourteen dollars.

I can't imagine how hard my arrest hit my father. His son, the son of a preacher, sent to prison for armed robbery. This time he withheld any more help, hoping jail would be a shock treatment strong enough to jolt me into a responsible life.

My case was processed faster than a used car dealer delivers a sales pitch. I pleaded guilty and was sentenced to three years, two on probation, and one to be served in the county jail. I was transferred to the county road camp in the Malibu Mountains.

I hated being restricted, but memories of my days behind bars are not of horror story caliber. The real horror is being in a stale-smelling cage where your every move is observed. The monotonous life is oppressive in its sameness, never broken by variety. So was the food. I will always remember the sticky oatmeal that glued itself to the dish, and the potato-laden stews.

35

There at the Los Angeles County Jail, prison life mirrored society; some prisoners were treated more equally than others. Take Bugsey Segal, then head of organized crime in L.A. His clothes were different from ours and so was his schedule. We wore blue denim. He wore silk shirts, pressed pleated trousers, and could often be seen outside his cell. My friends and I did a lot more pick and shovel work than he did, too.

After a year's worth, I was a free man and went home. I reveled in my freedom for a couple of weeks, then took a job at UCLA in the Building and Grounds Department. I filled my extra hours by being a part-time student in science and math. I rejoined the church and was active in youth programs at Hollywood Presbyterian Church.

In the midst of a welcomed and stable layover in life, I was interrupted along with every other American. Pearl Harbor exploded.

I was drafted in January 1942, and assigned to Camp Callan near San Diego. I instantly saw the army as a chance for forgetting my prison experience and forging ahead in a new discipline. My goal, perhaps the first ever, was to make sergeant. I was a model draftee during my three months in basic training. My aptitude test revealed my interest in math and I was asked to become an officer candidate. No one mentioned my prison record, and I certainly didn't bring it up. I was accepted as officer quality and sent to Wilmington, North Carolina. I figured to be found out at some point and bounced. Until then, I'd make the most of it.

Toward the end of my course nightmares plagued me. I'd relive the same scene each night: at the last moment before graduation an officer with a piece of yellow paper with my prison record on it would order me to step out of line. Then I'd wake up.

It never happened in real life. I breezed through,

graduated first in my class, got a second lieutenant's gold bars and the assignment I'd requested: the 37th Brigade, an antiaircraft brigade with the Fourth Army in California.

My superiors paid attention when I mentioned my interest in electronics and communications. I was put on top secret radar work. Radar detected targets then, but couldn't direct artillery. It took three men to aim the gun. I worked out a mechanism for radar to calculate and send a message to aim the gun. I modified army equipment to make my model, knowing it was against regulations, but nothing else was available.

As I was being chewed out by a captain, the commanding general walked by. The captain told him what I'd been up to. A day later the general called me into his office where he offered me a job as a signal officer.

Army life picked up. I took charge of radar and communications with the title, Signal Officer in Charge of Tactical Communications and Radar Defensive Network. Promotions gushed. I would just get used to a new rank and I'd be propelled to the next. I was made captain in two years.

That's where my ascent as an officer stopped. The commanding general's request to jump me to major generated shock waves of dissension among the men passed over. I never metamorphosed to major. The army career I'd carefully built crumbled. I was caught in the same trap that I went to jail for in L.A., my Robin Hood mentality, and with the same results.

In the army I was relatively innocent, although I did give people things that didn't belong to me. I got to be known as a soft touch for guys who wanted to buy items like cars and refrigerators at military rates. I would sign priority forms even though I wasn't authorized to do so. There's the weak defense that others were doing the same thing for their buddies, and they were, but that doesn't excuse anything. A disgruntled officer who was opposed to my speedy promotions over him found out and turned me in.

I had also been generous with army film projectors. I borrowed them for a program at Hollywood Presbyterian Church without the formality of getting permission, although I fully intended to return them. After an investigation, I was charged with misuse of government priorities and misappropriation of government property. That translates to "theft."

I was sent to March Air Force Base where I was tried by court martial. I thought I'd be kicked out of the army, which was upsetting enough, but I wasn't at all prepared for their decision. They hit me with the maximum sentence: ten years at hard labor and the expected dismissal from the army. The Ninth Corps of the Army subsequently cut my sentence to five years, to be served at McNeil Federal Penitentiary in Washington state. Anyone severed from the army, and especially by court martial, is due a presidential review of his case. Mine was delayed because government justice slowed when President Roosevelt died. Six months minced by, and then my case came up. I was pardoned by President Truman and ordered to Fort Leavenworth, Kansas, for rehabilitation.

The following year I traveled for the army, lecturing around the United States on radar. At the end of the teaching tour, I was honorably discharged. Once again, I had landed precariously on my feet. Once again, I went home. I opened my electronics company in Hollywood and continued a courtship barely begun before my second jail sentence. The girl was Alice Park. She knew I had been in the army, but not that I'd been in the army penitentiary.

Alice remembers our first meetings more clearly than I. And happily, after twenty-six years of marriage, her descriptions flatter me.

"I had seen him from a distance many times, and couldn't wait to meet Jim. The night I did meet him was at a church sing. He didn't pay any attention to me. There wasn't much reason to. I had two strikes against me because I'm ten years younger than Jim. That didn't bother me however. I remember telling my father, 'That's the man I'm going to marry.' What did stand in my way was Jim's engagement. Soon after I had pointed him out to my father as his future son-in-law, Jim became engaged to the minister's daughter._

"I would occasionally get a ride with him to a church function. I started off in the back seat. I did move up to the front, but nothing more. All I could do was adore him from afar.

"I had heard the church gossip that the engagement was off, and then out of the blue, in 1944, I got a valentine card from Jim who was now in the army. I was delighted and started writing frequently. I never knew that his letters were coming from jail. They arrived postmarked from all over the country. In 1946 he was in town and called for a date. I had just graduated from high school and was working in Hollywood where we met. We were married on my birthday, in 1947."

My father married us. We drove to New York on our honeymoon. I decided to include a few detours along the way to try to peddle some electronic equipment. I thought that the police across the country might be interested in my impulse indicator. That's the device I invented while working with the Los Angeles police.

The first stop was Pittsburgh. I journeyed into the old-fashioned building at police headquarters, equipment in hand, and asked for an audience with the superintendent of police.

"Nobody gets in to see him without an appointment," sneered the desk sergeant.

"How about his assistant?"

"You'll have a wait." The sergeant ignored me, hoping I'd just go away. I waited around two or three hours before he barked my name and pointed to the assistant's cubby. Then I went into the tiny office where

39

I demonstrated the impulse indicator. The assistant hadn't seen anything like it and called in the superintendent. I gave a second demonstration. They bought the indicator. At the conclusion of our visit, the superintendent invited Alice and me to dinner. He said he couldn't join us, but he'd be happy to arrange a tour of the city for us before dinner. Our chauffeur was the desk sergeant, suddenly the world's most polite gentleman. That reception in Pittsburgh spoiled me for the rest of the trip.

The New York Police couldn't be bothered. Department heads in St. Louis were cordial, but cool. And the FBI in Washington, D.C., was an experience in itself. It was my last stop on the round trip home. The FBI was interested in the indicator and asked to keep the device for a short time. I left it. Months went by. The FBI didn't reply or return my device. I called and was informed that they weren't interested at that time. I asked for it back and it was delivered by an unidentified messenger. I later learned that the bureau duplicated the device. That adventure ended my interest in selling and marketing my inventions. I decided to stick to Hollywood and my own electronics work.

4

Chapter

When St. Louis Andy, Mickey Cohen's friend, strode into my office I thought he was a bit player in a grade B gangster movie. He was short and dark with Groucho Marx eyebrows and a classic Brooklyn "dees," "dem," "dose" accent. I had to work to understand him. But after five minutes I rooted out enough data to know he was for real.

Andy's racket was betting on big horse races across the country. Like any businessman, Andy was interested in increasing his profits and, indeed, had thought up a way.

He had dropped by to probe my interest in making a "gadget" to execute his plan. Andy's fantasy was to hold the horse race results back from the Continental Wire System for ninety seconds. The system transmitted the winners to major cities all over the country. Andy wanted to flash the victorious horses' names to a legman

41

planted in a betting room, ready to bet the winner before the wire system relayed the information. The bookmaker, not knowing a race had ended, would take the bet on the number one horse. Andy would always bet a sure winner.

He delivered his plan in earnest, hushed tones. Though his words weren't in proper English, they made a lot of sense. I wasn't at all sure I could do it, but if we could set up his plan, it would make us a lot of money. Visions of big wins egged me on to construct a machine to do Andy's trick. I moonlighted this job while working for Cohen. It took four months to refine the teletype equipment and the electronic components. They worked, and we chose Arizona for our first location.

It helps when you can hold ninety seconds of the future in a vacuum. We always won! We were such a success that Andy wanted to open up the business over the whole country, like a McDonald's hamburger franchise.

We were having a drink in a bar on Washington Boulevard when Andy decided to head for St. Louis where he would be able to intercept all races west of the city. As we sat there, Andy doled out tickets and expense money for our November 10 date in St. Louis.

Setting up Andy's machine was, in my mind, like planting the seeds that would yield a guaranteed income. It's not easy to bet a sure winner each time. Andy's lopsided reasoning went, "Bookmaking is illegal, so what if they go broke because of us."

I knew we'd have it made financially once Andy's operations blossomed, but I began getting edgy. Pressures piled up. I kept a quicker pace. I pushed ahead like a bulldozer to ready Andy's St. Louis date and continue the Cohen jobs. On the home front, Alice was about to bring a new life into the world. I started to wonder, can I account for mine? For the first time in my life I had trouble sleeping. I'd lie down but spring back up, eyes open as an owl's. Longer chunks of time ticked away before I'd be able to close them and rest, refreshing myself for the next day's run.

The excitement of setting up the St. Louis deal with Andy ran out as fast as my drink at the bar. No matter which way I turned I couldn't shake the cloud of gloom hovering overhead. I can't explain why but Sunday, November 6, 1949, was to be the day I gave my life to Christ. I've dissected and examined that day and cannot unlock the combination that made me *hear* and *act*.

It began as a blue Sunday. First, in my effort to help with breakfast, I ended up burning the toast. Later Madeline toppled and scraped her foot while crawling to get a ball I'd tossed to her. It wasn't serious, but our game ended with her in tears. After lunch we stopped by Alice's parents and deposited Madeline with my mother-in-law. Alice and I wanted to pay our last respects to an uncle who died unexpectedly. As we left the funeral home my already grumpy mood darkened, so we decided to get away from the flagging day and drive to the beach. Fog frosted the coast with a dreary dampness that was even more depressing than my mood. We didn't even bother to get out of the car. Instead, we headed to a drugstore, picked up a paper to check the movie section, and opted to see *Pinkie*. Instead of watching the laugh riot I bargained for, I sat in the darkened theater facing a thought-provoking film. I had decided to pay a Sunday visit to friends in order to save our day. No one was home, anywhere. I even stopped by Cohen's, something I normally wouldn't have done with Alice. But no Mickey. Okay, I knew where I'd find some others. I wondered why I hadn't thought of the bar on Washington Boulevard sooner. At least Andy would be there. Only he wasn't. The place was so empty it echoed.

Driving in southern California has always been an

43

obsession with the natives, so we cruised. Our aimlessness got on my nerves. I felt frustrated that our day had gone so strangely, that we tripped every time we had taken a step.

Alice did her best to cheer me, chattering, planning for the new baby. One of her suggestions was to visit Billy Graham's tent meetings she'd been reading about. The papers had been covering Graham closely because a flock of celebrities had come forward to follow Christ. I thought it was a good publicity angle.

I had heard about Graham on the car radio, this young man who, in a short time, had been able to infuse people with excitement and turn them to Jesus Christ. Church rallies and functions were nothing new to me, but I was a little curious about this man. Why not see what was going on at Graham's canvas crusade? The day was wasted anyway.

The parking lot outside the tent on Hill Street was packed. When we entered, my mouth dropped open. The 6,500 seats were filled. The standing room was cramped. By the end of the series some 350,000 people would come to the crusade. There was a ripple in the line as thoughtful people cleared room for Alice to sit down. I couldn't pin a label on the group, though I wanted to. The people were as varied as the letters in the alphabet. Some were dressed up, some were in work clothes. I listened to familiar songs, stood up with the crowd, but kept my mental distance. I was just an observer.

My eyes followed the counselors as they singled out the people ready to go forward. A counselor would lightly tap the person on the shoulder and offer his aid. Then he would lead the convert to a separate tent and reassure him that this decision was the best of his life. They'd talk about the convert's future, answering the question, "What do I do now, how do I put feet to my faith?"

44

Not me. I flashed leave-me-alone messages like a kid who doesn't have the answer when the teacher is about to call on him. Someone rose to my challenge of hands off. I tensed when "Uncle Billy" Scholfield gripped my arm. I didn't know what to do. I was ready to toss him when he sensed my violence. He bowed his head to pray. Then, up from the center platform vaulted Billy Graham's voice, coming straight at me. "There's a man in the audience tonight who has heard this story many times before and who knows it's time to make a decision. He has been fighting his commitment, saying no to God. He may leave without Christ, and this may be the last opportunity God will give him to decide for Christ."

That was me he was talking to. I shifted, pushing down my troubles, my need for Christ, as I had for years. I believed in God, that Christ is the Son of God, so I'd be on safe grounds as far as eternity was concerned. Yet my mind felt as if it was in the midst of an earthquake, torn in two directions. I kept trying to convince myself that I didn't need to right my life as a man, as a Christian. Not now. I managed to go to church, if only occasionally, to put a phony froth over the truth of my working for Andy and the syndicate.

Still, Graham pried into my mind and urged, "You just can't decide for Christ whenever you think it's time. The time is when the Holy Spirit of God has brought conviction to your heart. If God is bringing conviction to you tonight, you dare not say no. This is your moment of decision."

The uncertainty and unrest of my life that I had kept submerged oozed up into my consciousness. I had no warning that in spite of all my resistance I'd whisper, "I'll go."

Scholfield walked me down the aisle of the crowded tent. Seeing the people packed inside, I realized we all had come for comfort of another sort, a comfort we couldn't get from our overstuffed chairs and lives. I walked down the aisle and out into a smaller adjoining prayer tent, Alice at my side. I was ready.

I had been schooled in religion and the Bible, but treated it like a history topic. Once inside the prayer tent, all those readings I'd skimmed, all those church messages I'd sat through—but hadn't heard—all that Christ meant came alive. It was as if someone had turned on an electric switch in the dark. I spoke to God. "God, if you think Jim Vaus means business with you, won't you mean business with Jim Vaus? If somehow you'll straighten out my life, all that I have is yours. I'll hold back nothing."

Alice had come forward with me even though she already had a working relationship with God. She couldn't know how these moments would change our life in every way.

As we left I ran into a newspaperman I knew from the days I worked with the police on the Brenda Allen case. He had followed my career and now recognized me as one of Cohen's men, not as a Christian. I wanted to dodge his questions and the inevitable publicity. I started to make a getaway but stopped midstream. His paper could tell the world about my change, that I had dedicated my life to Christ. It did the next morning under the headline, "Wiretapper Vaus Hits Sawdust Trail." The same story also told Alice, our families, and neighbors just what I'd changed from.

"I didn't know how involved he was," Alice remembers. "So the initial commitment really didn't make that great an impression on me. He said he would do better, but I had no idea better than what. Jim had been upset and had trouble sleeping. Ordinarily this man sleeps more soundly than a hibernating bear. When we left the tent I sensed a great relief in Jim's life, like he had put a heavy load to rest. I'll never forget how peacefully he slept that night.

"I hadn't worried or been concerned about Jim's work. I knew he had an electronics business and had branched out to detective work. He shared those stories with me. That night I found out there were many he hadn't. I certainly didn't learn everything the first night. We took it a day at a time. Jim's other life was in the past. I knew he was sincere and together we could do anything. I never gave our new life a negative thought, although I didn't realize how much it would change. I'm glad, but it is strange to see everything you own disappear."

All I was sure of after my decision was that I wanted to pursue God's path, not my own selfish one. I didn't have a blueprint, there was no time to plan, and nothing in my life was standing still. The day after my conversion, our first son, Dennis, was born. Alice knew about the syndicate, the thefts, and the income tax evasion. She also knew I had changed. Twenty-one years old, having just given birth to our second child, Alice responded with support so solid I thought we just might make it.

5

Chapter

I called Mickey Cohen to tell him about the decision. He hadn't read the paper yet and assumed, I suppose, as everyone else did except Alice, that I had my own reasons for wanting the notoriety. (I never have figured out what I would have gained, except fame as a crackpot, if I had staged that sort of crazy stunt.) Later that morning I drove to Cohen's house to try to get through to him how my life had changed.

"I couldn't figure Jim coming to my house that time of morning to tell me about Billy Graham," Cohen says.

"When Jim first told me about him, I thought he was talking about a prize fighter. There was a lightweight fighter in those days called Billy Graham. But this Graham, I didn't know who he was. It was a real shocker to me.

"When he first came to tell me about this experience, I didn't understand what he was saying. He said he was going to become a Christian. I said, 'Jim, what are you talking about?' I thought

anyone that was a gentile was a Christian. I said, 'What have you always been? You've been Christian.' Then when he said you have to give your life to Christ, and you really aren't a Christian before that, I thought it was a beautiful thing. I remember hoping he was talking true and saying to him: 'Jim, I want you to make me a promise. Promise me you'll never go back to the old way of living. Hang on to what you've got. It's wonderful. A lot of guys aren't going to like it but if the whole world turns against you, remember there's one little Jew right here that thinks the world of you for the decision you made and the guts you have for standing up for it I headed to my dresser and fished out some cash. I tried to give Jim $2500–4000, whatever I could lay my hands on real quick so he could get started on this new life of his. He pocketed what I already owed him, no more. He said, 'The Lord will take care of me.' I just looked at him. I hoped it would work for him, but I didn't understand these things."

It's true that Cohen didn't understand, but he accepted my new life and let me go. He wanted to meet Graham, maybe to make sure I wasn't kidding him.

Billy Graham met with us in Cohen's house a couple of days later. No one was around, which was unusual for Cohen. He had given the staff the night off. We hadn't been there more than a half hour and the phone interrupted. An AP reporter was on the line hunting down some possible copy. "Is it true Billy Graham is with you at home, Mr. Cohen?"

"No," retorted Cohen, "and if that guy came around I wouldn't let him in anyway." He hung up.

Our encounter was a little strained. Cohen was anxious, trying to do the correct thing for Graham, but the etiquette escaped him. Cohen offered drinks, Graham accepted a Coke. We somehow groped our way over barren chatter into interesting dialogue. We were readying to leave when all at once Cohen jumped up and began scurrying around. After much peering into cabinets and shelves, Cohen finally found what he'd been hunting. It was a Bible the government of Israel had sent him in thanks for some money he donated. Cohen wanted Graham and me to know that he, too, had a Bible.

On the way to the door, Cohen and Graham planned their strategy should the AP reporter follow up the story. They agreed to stick to "no comment." Sure as the morning sun, the reporter was on the job. He phoned Graham at dawn, "I've been talking to Cohen," he tried, "and he says you were at his place last night. Is this true?" Graham, still groggy, took the question seriously and answered, "If Mickey says so, it's true." We hit the headlines again.

6 Chapter

St. Louis Andy wasn't at all interested in my changed life because it changed his, too. My call to him was a painful one, nothing like my talk with Cohen.

"Andy, it's Jim. I have to tell you our deal is off."

"Jim, what's up, what do you mean?" Andy sputtered. "You want more money?"

"It has nothing to do with money, Andy. I've made a decision and I'm changing my way of life. I've dedicated myself to Christ."

"Christ? What about our set-up? Who's going to work the electronic stuff on the races?" raged Andy. His beautiful money-making scheme was falling apart.

"It's not going to be me. My old life's over. It's not because I don't want to work for you, it's just that I'm quitting the syndicate."

We went a few more rounds until the idea that I wasn't going to step off the plane next week in St. Louis sank in. He liked it less the more I talked. I sure didn't like the way we ended.

"You show in St. Louis or we'll be out to see you. Got it, Jim?"

"Andy, I'm not coming."

"No one quits on me, Jim. We'll see you."

With that we hung up, but I couldn't shut out his ominous threat.

I found other things to fill my thoughts. I looked to the Bible for wisdom. My mind absorbed the words. I thought about them, dwelled on them. I became certain that my key to Christianity was belief. I sifted out the word *believe*. Christ spoke Aramaic, he was recorded in Greek, and we're trying to know his works through still another translation, English. Do we grasp the meaning of "he who believes in me"?

I tracked down the word believe in Thayer's Greek Lexicon. I studied for days trying to tear down the fences separating me from what Christ truly meant when he said, "Believe in me." I mulled over meanings while shuttling between home, seeing Alice and Dennis in the hospital, and Graham's crusade. I needed closeness with my family, with Graham and his men while trying to get my bearings with God.

To believe for me was more than accepting the Bible as truth of the reality of God or Christ. It was a submission to the authority of Christ. Anything short of total invasion by Christ wasn't salvation. I had to obey God actively.

Days passed and then a week. Alice and Dennis came home. Together again with our firstborn, Madeline, we felt the promise of a fresh start. Before we could pull ahead, we had to get out of the rut I'd got us stuck in. It was time for restitution. I liked being a good provider. I had been making $60,000 to $70,000 a year and we had all the status symbols proclaiming a good

54

life. A nice home, pretty furniture, and a fancy car. We liked them. We'd even managed to save a little. Then I remembered all the people I'd cheated out of money and merchandise. I knew then that I had to repay every last cent and it was as simple as a bird molting feathers to let it go. Molt we did. By the time we finished, we had shed the car, the furniture, the house, and our savings account.

One day we were in the thick of straightening out our lifestyle when I heard a car motor. I saw the long black automobile glide close. It was too late if I had even wanted to make a getaway. Andy and his three henchmen blocked the driveway. I couldn't let them in the house with Alice and the children. As I stepped out into the patio, the only weapon at my side was my newfound trust in the Lord. There wasn't a thing to do but start talking.

"Andy, what do you think of my change?" I said and tried to smile.

"Ha, whatya talking about. You and that guy Graham are in it together. What's he paying you, anyway? I came to talk about our job," said Andy.

His men shifted restlessly.

I talked for my life and told Andy what happened. I told him I wasn't afraid because the Lord was looking out for me. The three thugs, standing still now like stumps, never got a word I said. But Andy, thanks to the Lord, heard me. In his words I'd "got religion."

"Jim, you mean all that stuff, don'tya."

"Yes, Andy, how about you?"

"What?"

"Why not come to one of Graham's meetings?"

"Jim, I got other business to take care of. So long. Let's go boys."

I'm sure those gorillas never understood why they had to leave, when they had clearly come to do a job.

I gave thanks to God that they didn't proceed with business as usual.

Ours was a case, as Alice says, of living by faith. I was set solidly in my conviction to pursue a straight course and pay restitution. Handing over money was easy, but trying to explain *why* never was. Every time I had to tell a man to his face that I had cheated him he would stiffen in horror as the story unrolled, staring at me with an incredulous look. I'd want to disappear. However, I'd stay and absorb the stare, then tell him I wanted to make good. Down to the last man, each accepted my story and not one pressed charges.

I went to the owner of the Bleitz Camera Company and explained that I had stolen his equipment by having it billed to Twentieth Century Fox Motion Picture Company. Don Bleitz just stared at me when I told him I was returning what I still had and offered to pay for the rest. He remembered the phony purchase order well enough; in fact, he had phoned the police about it. I wondered if he would again. Instead, he gave me a figure, and I wrote him a check. My explanation of why I returned his equipment, that I wanted to right myself with God, was so simple it was hard for him to believe.

I wrote to another company I'd swindled, Warner Brothers Broadcasting Corporation and told them what I'd done. I asked for an interview to work out payment. They replied that my letter was itself payment in full as far as they were concerned. Their reaction was hard for me to believe. I continued until all my debts were paid, and there were many. I never had repaid the woman who helped me replace the college's funds. She died before I had finished. At the time, that had seemed like a good reason to avoid paying it, but now I went back and put the balance in her estate.

I arranged for a long delayed date with the Internal Revenue Service. I was sure this debt would make the others look like peanuts. I hadn't reported the greater part of my income for years. My Hollywood clients who employed me to wiretap didn't send W-2 forms with payment, and Cohen paid me in cash. But the IRS was more interested in my information about Cohen than in my money. I talked to them about him, but since I wasn't privy to Cohen's accounts, I couldn't come up with many facts.

Restitution was expensive: $15,000 and worth it. Paying that off was a breeze compared to what I might have to do when I told the courts how I had perjured myself before the grand jury. I was scared. Righting the course of my life could land me in jail again. When I wrote to the district attorney's office admitting I perjured myself when I testified against Sergeant Jackson, I knew I'd be putting myself in a tight corner. The mob boys who testified with me against Jackson wouldn't be too happy about what I had to say, and it might get me tossed back behind bars for admitting my guilt. The day of the hearing the courtroom drew a crowd ready for some entertainment. Then, as the trial was about to begin, the Lord sent strength. Billy Graham's friend Cliff Barrows came in along with his father. "Jim, we heard about it so we came to pray," Cliff said.

The only privilege I asked for was permission at the close of the hearing to tell the source of my change, my reason for being in the courtroom.

We proceeded. I stood like a target as the questions were thrown like pointed darts. I answered every one and, at the day's end, I told the court the reason I had returned and altered my testimony: because I had accepted Christ as my personal Savior.

Sergeant Jackson was released from false charges, the syndicate laid low, and I have yet to be indicted for perjury.

Our life continued to be pulled together by a series

of miracles. When our bank balance was down to $5.00 and we needed groceries, the total came to $4.89. When the gas tank was empty, friends at church tucked a five-dollar bill into my pocket. When the car was gone, they offered me rides. The same happened when we sold the house. A church member, Jim Thornbury, offered us a house he owned but wasn't using.

It was hard for me to accept all the helping hands. In the past I had been the one to offer another a ride, a gift, a loan. It bruised my pride to be on the receiving end. One of my first lessons was to learn to be grateful, to know I wasn't the one in control.

7 Chapter

The daily invitations for me to speak at churches, clubs, schools, and independent organizations became a frame for our future. Interest snowballed. Requests for me to talk about my conversion trickled in at first, then the trickle became a stream. Speaking to groups soon turned into my new full-time job. I was booked for eight months, then a year in advance.

One of the first groups to hear my story was the Christian Businessmen's Committee in Hollywood. When I finished, a woman wearing a pink suit stood up and introduced herself as an assistant in the mayor's office. She said she enjoyed my talk and that she had read of my conversion. Then she went on to tell me what my destiny would have been if I hadn't responded to Graham's urge, "This is your moment of decision." She explained. "According to the FBI information that came into our office, a rival gang was set up to get you in St. Louis on November 10. You wouldn't have been alive to tell us about that, Mr. Vaus."

During my years of speaking I've been privilged to appear from time to time with Billy Graham. I thoroughly enjoyed those times. He's the most transparently honest man I've ever met. His outstanding personality and his sincere dedication have been an inspiration to me.

In the early days before Graham built his organization, I traveled with him and two brothers, T.W. and Grady Wilson, who are still his closest companions. I went with them on the Oregon crusade a few months after my conversion. We drove up through Yellowstone Park and on into Portland. The Portland appearance was a landmark in Graham's life; it was then that he decided to go on national radio with his "Hour of Decision" program. This decision settled his role as a national figure, set apart by God for the task he was doing. After the first program he had to open a two-man office to handle the mail that came barreling in. Today, five hundred people work in Graham's Minneapolis office.

I thought I had a gimmick to help Graham the night he premiered his "Hour of Decision." It was a wireless microphone. Graham likes to move around the stage while speaking to an audience. The thought of walking around free from the fear of getting tangled in microphone cords intrigued him. The mike clipped onto his tie, and the power unit attached to his belt. The antenna that went down the side of his leg was hidden by his trousers.

Now, no one is more gracious, publicly and privately, than Billy Graham. I had never seen him even slightly angry with anyone. But that night after the program, he marched me back to his dressing room and told me off in no uncertain terms. He informed me that the tip of the rubber-covered antenna wire was exposed. Every time it hit his leg, which it did a lot during the program, the exposed tip let out an electric shock. I was chagrined.

The next morning I awoke to find a note slipped under my door. "Please forgive me for my anger. I couldn't love you more if you were my own brother. Billy." I'm the one who should have been apologizing, but that's the kind of person he is.

As I continued to travel and speak, I repeated the tale of my conversion so many times it started sounding like a recording. I wanted to freshen my message so I began using electronics as a tool to expose the unseen, unheard proximity of God. With ultraviolet and black light I could show brilliant colors glowing in a gray granite slab. Black light picks up many things unseen in ordinary light. One is lipstick traces. I could both amaze and embarrass young people with that light.

I told a young man in front of a college audience that he'd had a date the night before. He had parked in a car and the girl sat on his right. It was very obvious she'd kissed him not once but many times. Although his face appeared clean, the pigment of the die from the lipstick remained in the pores of the skin and showed up under the black light. It brought a roar from the audience. It was a good beginning for a talk about how difficult it is to hide from the eyes of God.

The discussion periods following my talks were often rich in revelations and rewards. People who had listened, seated in uncomfortable folding chairs, would come and talk to me. I wasn't a priest in an ivory tower. I was a man who'd seen life from many angles, who couldn't condemn people for tripping up in a thicket of imposed "dos" and "don'ts." I had fallen hard myself, and I was a guy they couldn't shock. I may have given people hope; I was a living example that there's no standard form to fill out to join the Lord.

I was honored that Dr. Torrey Johnson, then pastor of the Midwest Bible Church in Chicago, arranged for me to be ordained. And I'll never regret that solemn occasion in July 1952. But the title invites images of a man more perfect than most, perched on a pedestal. I know I'm imperfect. I can't say I never get mad, never scream, never say or do anything to hurt others. I make mistakes. I fail. If I had to do it over again, chances are I'd be just plain old me, rather than Rev. Jim Vaus.

A more important reason for my apprehension is the fact that I'm not trained as a counselor. A minister today should have a full college education and go on to seminary and do graduate work in guidance counseling. It's a powerful and awesome responsibility to be dealing with people's lives. A minister needs as much training and guidance as he can get. I like to help people with whatever problems I can, but I'm nagged by the knowledge that I'm not qualified. I do as much as I'm able, then send persons to another clergyman, medical doctor, or psychiatrist for additional help.

8

Chapter

Home became a stopping place between trips. Sometimes I didn't even open my suitcase. When my schedule started getting ridiculous, Alice and I decided that instead of *my* racing home for a hurried time with my family that we'd move our home to me. It was a thirty-five-foot trailer. Lugging that thing behind us lacked charm as we crisscrossed the country in a crazy quilt pattern, but it was worth it to be together. For a while, that is. Then our life in the trailer got to be more of an irritation than an adventure.

Alice would get stuck in strange places with the kids, without a yard for them to play in, without neighbors or friends for company. When our third child, Steve, was due, we concluded that it was time to return to living in a house on solid ground. We found a perfect one, the house I grew up in. We bought it from my parents in 1952. It was terrific for the family but, unfortunately, I went back to being part-time husband and father.

There's not much glamor in dashing across the country living out of a suitcase. However, this was the way to reach people and that made it exciting. There were times when I felt drained, dragged out, but with a good night's rest I was ready the next morning. I felt strained and fatigued when, after weeks away, I was finally heading home. I was so anxious to get there I drove nonstop from Maryland to Los Angeles. The next day I still felt as limp as a deflated balloon. I was moving my heavy equipment out of the kids' way in our garage when my knees buckled. I knew it was something more than fatigue. My doctor called it polio.

Sister Kenny confirmed his diagnosis in the El Monte hospital. This kind woman, who had dedicated herself to rehabilitating polio victims, told me I would walk after a year, but that I would be a cripple. Knowing that I would walk someday helped. However, as I lay there, my paralyzed legs tucked between clean white sheets, I couldn't help wondering how much the disease would change my life.

Of course I had to cancel meetings I was scheduled to attend. The program I was most disappointed about missing was the one at Moody Church in Chicago. It was just four weeks away. Alice wrote a note about my situation and canceled my appearance. Four days later I got the church's answer: "We believe God will take care of you. Continuing to advertise your series. See you then." Billy Graham got word of my problems and asked people listening to his radio program to pray for me.

I didn't leap out of the hospital bed kicking my heels together, but I did have a rapid recovery. I went home in less than a month. A day or two later I was loaded, complete with wheelchair, on a plane headed for Chicago. When I landed I was too embarrassed to arrive in that wheelchair because I didn't think I really needed it. It wasn't easy, but I came off that plane walking. The only trace of polio left is that I've had a slight limp ever since.

From the day Billy Graham talked to me in his tent, he continued to be a tremendous influence upon my life. I kept trying to tuck myself under his umbrella. I carefully tried to mimic his life. I wanted to help people as he had. In 1955 I set up the Jim Vaus Evangelical Association to parallel the Billy Graham Association. However, my organization evolved away from being a copy of Graham's and became a nonprofit corporation to support a second one, Missionary Communications Service (M.C.S.). Its object was to put marooned missionaries in touch with the rest of the world through electronics. It was a way for me to use my know-how in this field. The same method I developed for St. Louis Andy in order to cheat bookies worked easily to bring messages from missionaries in isolated regions—mostly in Africa and South America.

The system was also used to transmit medical advice. For example, local doctors were scarce. A doctor had many miles to cover, and he couldn't possibly visit each remote village. That left the villages without medical care. But a doctor could serve a village by remote control, so to speak. He could listen to the symptoms and then prescribe medicines for the diseases he had diagnosed. He could coach a midwife while she was delivering a child. The service also offered a village news and information, and gave the people a voice.

M.C.S. also gave me a project into which I could funnel the surplus from the money I received as payment for speaking. I've never believed the saying that "poverty is cousin to virtue." But when I took in several thousand dollars a month I wanted to share what I had.

Putting the systems into the out-of-the-way places was simple compared to the problems of getting to those places in the first place. No matter where I went, I found the last fifty miles to be the toughest.

After we had gone as far as we could by plane, I'd hop aboard whatever transportation showed up. In Yarinacocha, Peru, it was a dugout canoe. It looked about the size of a boat a kid plays with in his bathtub but it didn't sink, although another quarter inch into the water and I would have been swimming. When I arrived the natives peered. I didn't try to keep my identity cloaked. Besides being a blue-eyed Caucasian weighing close to three-hundred pounds, I had on a business suit. After being given a generous welcome and a dinner I couldn't identify, I was assigned a grass hut built on stilts. My bed was a bag and a blanket of mosquito netting. By this time I was used to appearing before large crowds, but the audience I drew at the foot of the hut gave me stage fright. They surrounded the hut and peered through the slats. I was the biggest white man they'd ever seen and they were there to get a look at me naked. I did my best to disappoint them by doing the quickest change I could manage and dove into my sleeping bag. The grass hut rustled.

I worked with M.C.S. from 1955 to 1957 but it was doomed to financial disaster. Though my speaking stints established the service, and I had a windfall from the book I wrote, *Why I Quit Syndicated Crime* (which became the basis for a movie about my life, *Wiretapper*, released in 1955), there still wasn't enough money to feed M.C.S. The clamor for money got louder as the project grew; I simply couldn't support the increased demands. Missionary Aviation Fellowship in California eventually absorbed the service and combined communication with aviation service for missionaries.

Would I work for the law or a gangster?
It was a simple decision.
Mickey Cohen offered more money,
and he paid in cash—no need to report it to the IRS.

I had heard about Billy Graham on the car radio,
this young man who, in a short time,
had been able to infuse people with excitement
and turn them to Jesus Christ.
I decided to go and see what was going on
since the day was wasted anyway.

Jim Vaus and Billy Graham

I began using electronics as a tool
to expose the unseen, unheard proximity of God.
By using ultraviolet and black light
I could pick up many things unseen in ordinary light.

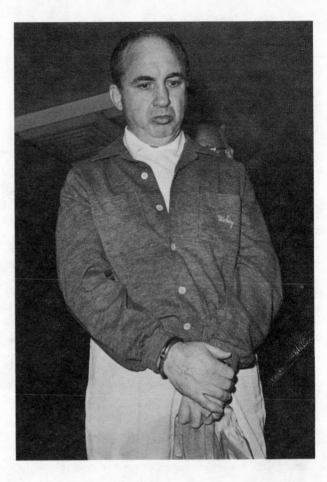

In 1951 I had to testify against Cohen.
He got five years.
When he was released
my insurance company got nervous
about how he might thank
his friends for testifying against him.
They canceled my accidental death insurance.

When Billy Graham
came to talk to the boys,
walk the streets with them,
and visit their families,
he led many to Jesus Christ.

Santy Lopez

Once in awhile a boy comes along
who is a leader, a mover.
Santy Lopez was such a boy.
Then it happened.
The call said Santy was dead, shot in the back.
The headlines the following day
told the story in brief:
"Slay Wrong Boy in Gang War."

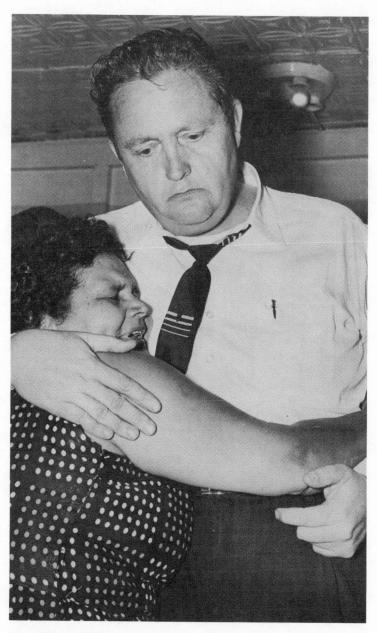

Mrs. Lopez and Jim Vaus

Mark Hatfield and family with Jim Vaus

When Mark O. Hatfield, then governor of Oregon,
came east he paid a visit to Y.D.I.
I couldn't help wondering aloud,
why couldn't a governor of a state that boasted
the largest lumber industry
come up with some lumber for our camp buildings.

Our empty acreage soon became Camp Champion
in honor of George Champion.
It was exhilarating to be there that first summer,
knowing that our open fires would be replaced
by a dining hall
and the tents by real cabins.

In 1959 we opened a storefront on 108th Street.
The main attraction was the beauty shop.
But it wasn't all lipstick and curlers. The girls
got into gang fights every bit as foul as the boys.

Over the years the camp has grown up
to be a combination of manicured manor
and natural wilderness. To the left, a small pond
reflects the clear sky. Then to the right,
like a gem in a perfect setting, is the chapel,
Its large windows curtained by the lace
of leafy trees and ferns.

Mickey Cohen is a part of my life.
He stopped being my boss in 1949.
He is still my friend, today.

Jim Vaus and Mickey Cohen

9

Chapter

I got a surprise in the mail about the same time I was trying to straighten out the money troubles of Missionary Communications Service. It was a subpoena to appear in court to testify against Mickey Cohen.

Cohen had been skirting juries for years when the inevitable occurred in 1951: he was charged with tax evasion and put up for trial. I was one of the hundred or so the Internal Revenue Service hoped could nail him. I didn't want to hurt Cohen, but all I could do was have faith and tell a straight story about what I knew, which actually wasn't all that much. Neither my testimony nor that of the others helped him. Cohen got five years. He served three and a half at McNeil Island Penitentiary. When he was released, my insurance company got nervous about how Cohen might thank his friends for testifying against him. They canceled my accidental death insurance policy.

Contrary to what the insurance men concluded, Cohen never retaliated against me. He explains why: *"Jim's all man, but it wasn't in his make-up to get involved in violence. It was my way of life. I came up in the ranks of the syndicate because I did what I was commanded to do. I thought it was dog-eat-dog and did my job . . . artistically. I never figured Jim in this category. He was kept in a certain category in my operations, different from other people. He wasn't a part of the inner circle. I never figured him to stand up in court. In fact, I told him before he went to testify, 'Look, I don't want you to lie.'*

"Now, there are some others who testified against me that I really have a bad grievance against. And some got hurt for testifying against me. But Jim and some others did what they were supposed to do. If I thought they were going to do differently, I was a fool."

When Cohen was released I was ready with help. Alice and I carried part of his rent, paid for his gas, and for a time I loaned him our Ford coupe. He had been generous to me and I wanted to repay him for the way he treated me after my conversion. What Cohen didn't tell me was that he already had a Cadillac. He accepted my car and used it, while I hitchhiked—'way before it became a popular sport.

I found out about the Cadillac from the boys at the Internal Revenue Service who told me I was being played for a sucker. I guess I was. I exploded. Cohen brought back the car along with some weak excuses.

In spite of little things like that, Cohen is a part of my life. I've got nothing to gain and lots to lose when people arch their eyebrows over my association with Cohen. Just knowing him brings questions: Am I still associated with the syndicate? Just what is my association with Cohen?

He stopped being my boss in 1949. He is still my friend, today.

I've never tried to cram religion down his throat,

but if anyone can keep him from becoming more deeply mired in a life of crime, it's me. If anyone can help him refocus his life, it's me. He trusts me and knows I won't lie to him. In order to get a message across you've got to win a hearing with the person, although conversion is God's responsibility.

Cohen goes to church to hear me speak occasionally. Once on the way back from church a policeman recognized Cohen and stopped us. "Where you been?" he wanted to know.

"We been to church!" Cohen couldn't resist shouting. It was true, but I don't think the policeman believed a word of it. He probably still doesn't.

10

Chapter

It was during one of my speaking trips that I met my administrative assistant, Betty Craig, at the Christian Youth Crusade in Washington, D.C. After the rally I went with a group to a restaurant and happened to ask if anyone knew of a good secretary. On the way out the door, Betty introduced herself and said she'd like to apply for the job. Betty's home was in Glasgow, Scotland, and she was working for the British embassy. I did some checking and found she was doing an excellent job. I hired her the next day. That was in 1957. In the years since, Betty has become an American citizen and means much more to my work than just a secretary or administrative assistant. She's my strong right arm.

"I'd listened to him speak," says Betty, "and was very impressed with what he said. I still am."

Gradually our house began to resemble an inn and we welcomed the many visitors. But I did grow weary of so many people inspecting my family and lifestyle like a store window display. Perhaps that's why when driving through Grants Pass, Oregon, on my way to Vancouver, B.C., I stopped at the *For Sale* sign parked in front of Paradise Ranch.

The name fit the one hundred peaceful acres. Why couldn't I come home to this, instead of the thoroughfare my Los Angeles home had become? I phoned Alice. She agreed to meet me at the ranch on my return trip in October 1957.

We moved in by Thanksgiving. I flew out the next day for presheduled meetings in London and didn't return until Christmas Eve. My schedule for the new year was even busier than the last. I've always treasured the quiet life of the ranch, but Alice is the one who had to live daily with the five children and fifty Black Angus. We also endured a tragedy here that soiled the beauty for us.

"I'd never seen a cow face-to-face when suddenly I found I was running a ranch," admits Alice.

"Our first morning there I sent our oldest son out to take the cows to pasture. Dennis was about eight and absolutely terrified. He had hardly got out the door when he came bounding back, tears building, wailing, 'The cows won't let me in the gate!'

"The children now think it was the best thing that ever happened to them, but for me there was something wrong with that move.

"It was lush, green, beautiful land, but I'm a city girl. We were thirty minutes from town and people. Jim was away even more of the time and I was so lonely. When the state highwaymen came by one night to report that my cattle were out on the road (my cattle?), I wondered, why am I into this? To make the hours pass I spent more time cooking. I started to bake bread which was the most fun. And in September 1959, Alissa Gayle was born.

"I had problems with her from the beginning. She had a convulsion when she was a few weeks old. The doctor at the local hospital didn't know the cause, but she was bleeding internally,

84

in her head. She seemed to recover and he sent her home. We were strengthened during this time by the Word of God, 'Yea though I walk through the valley of the shadow of death, I will fear no evil for thou art with me.' There are rich treasures to be had in the dark hours, blessings that the light can never reveal. At home the sickness intensified. I took her to Portland for treatment. The staff explained her symptoms: fluid was building up in her head. I got my hands on a medical book and looked up the problem. I was sure she had hydrocephalus, water on the brain. Today, that disease can be cured but in 1959 it still mystified the medical profession. We shuttled her to Portland for seven operations, but they didn't help. She lost her sight, then her hearing.

"Up until then we had prayed asking the Lord to give us back our little girl, but I remember kneeling at the side of her empty crib and softly asking, 'Not our will but thine be done.' Sweet peace filled my heart. I knew that whatever our loving Father decided would be acceptable.

"We could not keep her with us, she was too sick, so we placed Alissa Gayle in a hospital. No words can tell what it was like to lay our baby in another's arms, somehow knowing we were not to have her again here on earth. On our way home from the hospital our oldest son expressed all our feelings when he prayed, 'Dear Lord, thank you for letting us have Alissa Gayle for a little while . . .'

"Jim was away, attempting to break through to kids in Harlem at this time. It became clear he was going to be based in New York. We needed to be pulled together as a family. It was time for another move. The doctors told us it would be best for the baby, and for us, if she stayed in Oregon. It was heartbreaking. Although she did need care, she didn't need us. I had a husband and four other children who did.

"When we left Paradise Ranch, Alissa Gayle was under the hospital's care and the watch of friends who visited her often during those painful months. Then she died and went to be with him who loved us so much that he gave his son."

During our time in Oregon I became friends with

Mark Hatfield, now a United States senator. When I met him, he was secretary of state for the state of Oregon. Later he became governor. I admired Hatfield as an honest young politician who was committed to Christ. I wished him well in his career.

I was invited to tour a state prison with one of Hatfield's associates. The idea of going back into jail gave me a chill. But this time was different; we got royal treatment. Going down the line meeting the staff, there was one introduction that was unnecessary. I already knew Warden Spires. He had been at McNeil Federal Penitentiary the same time I had, on the other side of the bars. He was a lot more fun to talk to this way.

That visit was the start of an avalanche of thinking I did about all those prisoners still locked inside their cages, especially the kids. My church cut me loose when I first got into trouble—just at the time I most needed guidance. Maybe I could help these kids some way.

I took every opportunity to talk to youngsters. Many had been penned up for years, for crimes it was hard to imagine anyone committing. I told them my story and about how I'd changed through Christ. The kids listened. We had something in common.

At Eastern State Penitentiary in Pennsylvania, after what I thought had been a particularly penetrating rap session, a boy with sad eyes came up, looked straight at me and said, "Mr. Vaus, it was a good talk you gave. But it would have been even better if you had talked to us about Christ before we got sent up. If you had, maybe some of us wouldn't have landed here."

My next stop after Pennsylvania was a meeting in New York City sponsored by Percy Crawford, a man noted for his work in youth programs. Church-going youngsters came to the meeting in droves. They were good kids and I could see they were getting something out of it. But the voice of that boy in jail kept running through my head like a broken record. How do you reach kids on the loose? They, more than any, need someone to gather them in and try to guide them before it's too late.

At the close of Crawford's meetings, I took a walking tour of Manhattan through the crisp April evening. I hadn't seen New York since our honeymoon nine years ago.

I started in Greenwich Village and worked my way uptown. I stopped at a Fifty-seventh Street newsstand for a rest. I noticed the cover of the current *Life* magazine; it advertised a story of several gangs that were terrorizing the city. I bought a copy and stood right on that corner and read every word of the article. It was chilling. The kids they talked about were, on the average, young, poor, black or Puerto Rican, kids no one would have paid attention to, except that they staged all-out wars on city streets. Wars were generally between rival gangs, but passersby got hurt, too, and occasionally were targets. According to that article, the problem was mushrooming like a black cloud over the city.

I looked up from the magazine. The city I saw was overcrowded with fur-coated, chic people who looked like they'd stepped out of a fancy Fifth Avenue store window. As I watched, and then walked, I thought about those kids condemned to a life where they were short of physical and spiritual nourishment. The only fur coats they saw were on rats.

The *Life* article served as an appetizer. These kids were satellites to a society that kept them distant, and ignored them, if possible. They deserved a wider choice of destinies than gang life held. If they didn't die in a fight, they'd be arrested for fighting, robbing, or murder. Maybe these were the kids to whom I could offer an alternative way of life. No one else seemed to be doing it.

I decided to stick around awhile and went to the

public library to research the rest of the story. I learned there were fourteen areas in New York dubbed especially high in crime. The top of this list, no position to be proud of, was the 23rd Precinct in Spanish Harlem, 96th Street to 119th, the East River to Central Park.

I took the subway uptown to get my own impressions. I walked these streets; they were far different from my midtown starting point. The city treated East Harlem like an appendix. It was thought useless and they'd just as soon cut it off. In many ways, it already had been. I took care where I stepped; the sidewalk looked and smelled like the garbage truck had been emptied on it. I heard whistles go off down the street like an alarm. It was because of me; the locals thought I was a policeman. I passed the post office. It was called Hell Gate Station, taking its name from a geographical area of Manhattan. Many years ago, people noticed that the Harlem and East rivers became very tempestuous where the two intersected. They called it the Devil's Boiling Pot. Later, they called it the Gate of Hell. The adjacent land was known as Hell Gate. The name describes the way it feels to live in that area.

The squalid, aloof, hostile, teeming square mile of East Harlem held out its invitation to me: Try, if you dare. It hit the nerve controlling my stubborn streak.

The next evening I spoke in a Times Square church and mentioned my concern for the youth of Harlem. An elderly woman on her way out tucked a note into my pocket and said, "Here's a man you should get in touch with." The name on the paper was Captain Conrad S. Jensen.

I looked again at the paper with Captain Jensen's name on it. I saw that he ran the 23rd Precinct of East Harlem. I phoned Jensen and told him that a woman at the meeting gave me the paper with his name on it. He chuckled. "That was my mother," he said. I asked for an appointment to talk about the gang troubles and the kids. He said he'd see me the next Monday morning.

I called Alice and told her I had been delayed a bit in New York, then returned to the library and boned up on the not-very-pleasant subject of juvenile delinquents.

Monday morning, I took my second subway ride to East Harlem's 103rd Street stop and walked to 104th and the police station. A polite desk sergeant directed me to Captain Jensen on the first floor. I explained to the captain, who was dressed in civilian clothes, that I was thinking of moving to East Harlem to try to work with the kids, to get them in touch with Christ. I noticed a Bible on his desk along with the piles of paper work and stack of reports. He replied, "I've been praying that God would send a man like you into this community."

Jensen talked to me about the kids and their gangs. Harlem kids come of age on the streets. That's where they get their education. It's their finishing school, literally for some. There's a slim line separating adolescence from manhood and the crossover age gets younger every year. Nine-year-old children hustle to survive; by thirteen some are fathers. Their territory may be drawn tighter than anyone else's on earth. Some people think they live in a city, or perhaps a neighborhood. These kids live on, in, over, one block. That block may house more people than many cities.

In the one-square mile that makes up East Harlem, 196,000 people compete for space. The raw energies frazzle nerves and invite violence. A Saturday night dance in a basement with a stolen jukebox relieves the sameness. So did the gang fights. Every fight meant trouble; some kid would get killed, then the defeated gang would retaliate. These kids, ages about fourteen on, developed sophisticated structures within the gangs.

89

They used anything they could carry as a weapon. Most of them knew how to make zip guns out of wood, rubber bands, and a piece of pipe. Some had real guns.

I wanted to get inside of this and offer something more. Something other than just a life that would end because of a murder, a suicide, a gang bop, an overdose or, if violence misses, grind out slowly on the skid row streets.

The first thing to do was to get a place where kids could come off the streets. My original plan was to make a work center where I'd teach them electronics.

I asked Captain Jensen if he had any ideas about where I could set up a club house, a place I could live in too. He said he knew where there was an empty storefront. It had been a florist shop but now it was really run down. I rented it immediately.

Jensen recommended a contractor, Arnold Thompson, to do the renovating. We met over lunch and then went to take a look. With each step, we risked falling through the rotted floor to the basement. I told Thompson what I wanted in the way of room. Some walls had to be removed. The windows invited break-ins, they'd have to go. So would the glass door. It seemed all that we could really use there was the address, 2110 Second Avenue. Thompson took on that task of making something out of a clump of old, moldy rooms in the center of a wasteland.

I had a few other arrangements to take care of. One was financing, and the other was explaining to Alice what I was about to embark on, when I wasn't all that sure myself.

En route to Oregon, I stopped in at Billy Graham's Minneapolis office and told his group what I hoped to do. They were enthusiastic and let me use the facilities to ready my initial fund-raising mailing. The results would tell me if there was to be support for my project.

I sent letters to people I'd met during my speaking years and to everyone else I knew.

Back home at Paradise Ranch, I told Alice of my plan. Perhaps she'd been through so much that nothing surprised her anymore. When I outlined what I wanted to do and where I wanted to do it, she took my news calmly. She readily agreed I ought to try to seek out Harlem's children, though she knew that she would have to run the ranch and the children alone over a long period.

I stayed a few days longer than I had planned to in Oregon to enjoy my family. The next separation would last awhile. I made sure Alice had enough money and that there would be ranch hands to help care for the livestock.

I loaded my electronic equipment and myself onto the 2½-ton truck and left early on a Sunday morning to make a speaking date at the First Baptist Church in Grants Pass, Oregon, fifteen miles away. What Alice didn't know when I pulled out was that I had left her all our cash and didn't even have enough to buy gas to New York, let alone meals.

That morning I told the congregation about the boy in jail who asked for someone to reach out for other boys and direct them before they, too, get into trouble. I told them my hope for Harlem, and about the storefront I'd rented for a start. When I was ready to drive off, a man came up to wish me luck, and though he didn't know of my need, handed me fifty dollars and said he'd also like to pay for the gas to get the truck to New York.

11 Chapter

When I drove up to 2110 Second Avenue, I was delighted. The windows were boarded up and reinforced with a six-inch wall. No one could break through that or the solid wooden door that replaced the glass one. 2110 would never resemble the Ritz, but Thompson managed to make a comfortable club out of that ramshackle string of tiny rooms. He started at the bottom and put in a new floor, paneled the walls, and painted the ceiling. He divided the back space into a bedroom, quarter bath, tiny kitchen. In front, he made a small office where you could talk to a kid alone. On back, there was a snack bar and the long laboratory bench I had requested for my electronic equipment.

For extra security I rigged up a closed circuit television to let me get a look at any visitors before letting them in. I combined this with a two-way intercom system, so I could talk without opening the door.

I got a detailed description of the local gang structure from Jensen with as many names and addresses as the police department had. I planned to follow up the names, talk to the boys, and try to interest them in coming over to the club.

I've never walked up and down so many flights of stairs for nothing. It was like blindman's bluff. I'd ask for a boy. "Never heard of him," or "He lives in the next tenement," were the usual avoidance techniques. When I'd get to the next door, no one heard of him there either. I couldn't get anyone to talk to me at all. A rumor took root that I was a cop. Others followed: I was an official from the government investigating the boys; I belonged to the crime commission; I was a leader of the Communist party, and my mysterious storefront with the blocked-out windows was a front for a communist cell.

At the time, my living quarters seemed like a cell. I set up a bed in the back. It was so cozy I hardly had room to move. Arnold Thompson often stopped in to see if I was surviving, bringing a couple of doughnuts and talk. He certainly was a welcomed sight. I didn't have many other conversations. I would stop and talk with Captain Jensen during work hours but, although he was cordial and helpful, he was a busy man.

I passed a few Sundays with a family I knew in New Jersey, the Krentels. So went the late spring, New York's pretty, if brief, season. My existence went downhill: lonely, lonelier, loneliest. Summer hit like dynamite and seemed determined to stick around forever. The air in East Harlem stood still. The sun baked the garbage-strewn streets. The stench waited in invisible ambush to attack the senses. No one moved.

The idle time almost did me in. This was one of the lowest points of my life, much worse than my jail stints. All I had to do was lock the door, say goodbye to Jensen, and no one would know the difference. Invitations for

me to speak all over the country beckoned. Some crit-
icized me for throwing my life away on people that
didn't care. My critics insisted when I had the opportunity to reach far greater numbers—opportunities to talk
to thousands—that I was being stubborn to confine
myself to just a few. What they didn't know was that
these few shunned me. I began to think that I should
quit, but decided against it as I contemplated the words
of E. Margaret Clarkson's hymn:

So send I you to labor unrewarded,
    To serve unpaid, unloved, unsought, unknown,
To bear rebuke, to suffer scorn and scoffing—
    So send I you to toil for Me alone.*

The one thing I did accomplish during this capsule
of unused time was to take a hard look at Harlem life.
There is real honesty in Harlem. Residents manage to
mingle and reach an agreement on coexistence without
fences, veils, or privacy. There's no place to hide. Two
rooms can house eight to ten people. Kids and parents
rotate using the beds, if there are any. The kids are
initiated to sex early so they see it as another part of life.
Harlem morals reflect this; an unwed mother is proud
of her baby. It's a status symbol. At first, the loose
morals amazed me. I was used to middle-class codes.
After being around for awhile, I began to understand
why people behaved the way they did, and to appreci-
ate them for what they were.

By September the air turned cooler. It was time for
the kids who had scattered during the summer to return
to school. I counted the school as my last shot. If I
couldn't get through to the kids at Galvani Junior High
School then I didn't have any more places to try. I

thought if I could put on an electronics show, I might catch their attention.

I wondered what kind of reception I'd get from the public school when I appeared out of nowhere, representing no one, and asked to put on my show. Captain Jensen's good word opened the door for me to talk to Edward Gersh, the dean of discipline.

"I had respect for the man," said Gersh. "I listened to his idea. He explained he wanted to try to interest some of the trouble makers in electronics, and help them establish better relationships with each other and the community. That would be some task. I knew what Jim was facing.

"I was the school disciplinarian, the bad boys were put into my class. When they came to class, I always had to search them. I would often find a knife taped to the side of a boy's leg. Kids sometimes came to school with loaded guns. In one year, nineteen or twenty out of a class of twenty-five ended up dead or in jail five years later. These were the kids Jim was after.

"After my first talk with Jim I knew he would be successful. He had the right instincts. I could see he was smart enough to learn how to work with the kids and that's important. Some people who have been around these kids over fifteen years still hadn't figured out how to get through.

"I introduced him to the principal, Israel Flax. We talked about his electronics show, his plans. When he left I said to Flax, 'What do you think, boss?' He said, 'I think so, Eddie.'

"We decided we'd go all out to help him. He had every quality except experience going for him. He needed some training, the same kind new teachers in East Harlem get. Flax and I gave him a double dose. He learned quickly. He had to.

"A week after we talked with Jim to tell him what to expect, he showed up driving this tremendous truck. He's a big man, but he didn't have any assistants to help unload that mass of equipment. 'Do you want some extra hands?' I asked. 'Don't bother, I got it,' he replied and unloaded thousands of pounds of electronic gear. He reassembled it onstage. And out of all that stuff came

a fantastic performance. The kids, who had started off with show-me expressions, loved it. We all did."

There was a lot riding on their response, so I did a full dress show. There was nothing subtle about it. I jolted them out of their sullen stares with marches played in stereo, a phenomenon that was still relatively unknown. The five-foot high speakers performed as grandly as they looked. The big hit was the recording of the railroad train traveling at lightning speed. It sounded like it was cutting through the auditorium, ripping it in half.

I recruited volunteers and projected their voices off beams of light, pumped lightning through a boy's body and let him light a fluorescent bulb with his fingertips. I demonstrated the hidden colors that black light brought out and all the other electronic wonders I could muster.

Then six months after I'd begun, overnight, kids flocked to 2110. They brought their friends. It got so crowded in that small storefront that I had to give out membership cards. And so Youth Development, Inc. was born.

12

Chapter

When Y.D.I. opened, the major neighborhood problem was gang wars. With the flip of an insult, a war was born—and they were vicious. Zip guns, chains, brass knuckles, and knives clashed, killing and wounding kids in the streets.

I wanted a crack at the tougher nuts with name tags like Bimbo, Dynamite, Dirty Louis, Blond Benny, Half-a-Chicken, who led gangs like the Dukes, Viceroys, Playboys, Dragons, Hawks, Red Wings, Untouchables.

Alone, these kids were helpless. They had found a way to make themselves powerful by binding together as a unit. Association with a gang gave a kid recourse if he was wronged or thought he was. For instance, if a guy wouldn't give his subway seat to a rival gang member's girl, she complained. The boyfriend couldn't do anything about it himself, but he could broadcast his grievance to his buddies. He'd tell his gang how the other guy insulted the girl. The seemingly insignificant incident, where almost nothing happened, could easily escalate into a war. Most gang wars or rumbles would start with a word, a movement, some small spark that flared up into a roaring fight. A guy simply "walking bad," or "looking bad," often got the winds of war blowing.

The formalities of war were as intricately detailed as the Pentagon's. These boys marked off territorial boundaries and sorted out rivalries and allies for the sport of war. Presidents and vice presidents, war counselors and prime ministers planned attacks and counterattacks as if it were a football game. But when the final words of war were uttered, "The shit is on," everyone ran for cover. No one knew what would happen next, who would get hurt, or who would die. Often, no one really knew why the war was on at all.

Tony Blondet, former gang leader, now a Y.D.I. staffer, remembers the days when, *"Gangs were the kids' world. It was hard not to belong. If you tried to be a loner you were a target. We weren't into the Third World thing yet. Our gang life was more just for us, not some cause. Belonging to a gang gave a kid an identity, a strength, an occupation. We had style, jackets with our names on them, a flashy way of walking. We used strategy for staging our wars. We didn't just run around bopping anybody.*

"I was president of the Playboys, just getting started when I was arrested on Park Avenue. We were on to a rumble and I had a sawed-off shotgun. I got sent up for twenty-eight months. When I got out, I went along with friends to Y.D.I. Vaus produced a place kids could be. He wasn't just another white social worker marking time between paychecks. He's had an impact on lives."

Though they were tough, the boys had little other than gang life. Some didn't have homes; some didn't have enough to eat. I reacted to their situations by being too casual about handouts at first. Gersh set me straight.

100

"The boys' families had been on relief for three generations," Gersh remembers. *"It was a way of life. These kids were used to people giving, hustling, taking away. They didn't expect much, but tried for what they could. The most important word with them is respect. You've got to win it, and you don't do that by giving them things. They think people who give them things are doing so because they're scared of them and are trying to buy friendship. They'll take what's offered, but won't respect the giver.*

"Jim got into some trouble with this in the beginning. A kid would borrow a quarter for food or to get somewhere. Fine. But then Jim would give him another the next time he asked. He found out that you can lend the money, but before you do it again, the first I.O.U. had better be paid back. Jim learned about that and right away showed the kids he was strong. They could carry 'pieces' and 'shivs', but they couldn't buffalo him. When Jim said something, he meant it, whether a kid had a weapon or not. I'm sure Jim thought 'What if the kid uses the knife?' but he kept cool. The kids respected him. He was there day and night with them. They realized he wanted to help and they responded to his love with their own kind of affection."

I quickly found out that electronics wasn't the answer. The kids I wanted weren't about to come into a class. I needed something else which would attract them. My electronics school did a quick change into a clubhouse. My prize was a pool table; that was the center of the action. From there, we structured a program of activities and lessons.

The mailing I sent out was bringing in around a thousand dollars a month; the center was active. And so Y.D.I. was beginning to be funded.

The board of directors was formed by a divergent group of men who came together and gave their talents to the management of 2110 Second Avenue. My early reputation wasn't exactly impeccable, and I knew I would need solid financial and legal help, as well as general advice. The first man I recruited was Arnold Thompson, the contractor who had made 2110 a haven.

I asked George "Gus" Lambrides, a certified public accountant, to act as treasurer, to handle all the money and write all the checks. The firm of Samuel D. Leidesdorf audited the accounts to see that the mandates of the board were carried out as originally ordered. Attorney Julius B. Poppinga was architect for Y.D.I.'s corporate structure and bylaws. He made application to the Internal Revenue Service asking them to rule that our contributions be tax exempt. Businessman Dave Swanson, one of the owners of Thomas' Bakeries, and his wife, Darlene, and Alex Sampson joined, bringing ideas and advice. At Y.D.I.'s conception, I was also a board member. I later decided that position invited a conflict of interests, since I was a paid employee.

Youth Development, Inc., was legally incorporated June 17, 1959. It was set up as a privately funded, nonprofit, nondenominational, nonpolitical corporation. "The object of the corporation is the promotion of the physical, social, cultural, and spiritual welfare of urban youth, the development of a vital godliness and a moral conscience among them, and the establishment and maintenance of a witness, to urban youth and others, for the gospel of Jesus Christ as revealed in the holy Scriptures."

When Y.D.I. became a fact, not a dream, it was time to get the family back together. Alice came out for a week and stayed with me at 2110. We scouted for a house and found a comfortable one in Tarrytown, north of the city, close enough for a quick commute. Having my family with me instead of wishing they were there made the Y.D.I., and life, much more of a pleasure.

It didn't take long to realize I needed help. I had more boys and activities than I could handle. I knew if I was going to accomplish anything in Harlem it wasn't going to be done alone.

I was looking for men to work with me at Y.D.I.

Jensen introduced me to Piri (Petey) Thomas who dropped by when I was in talking to Jensen at the precinct. Thomas was just out of Sing Sing where he had served a sentence for armed robbery. He landed a job as a foreman in a bakery and was determined to clean up his life with Christ's help. Petey knew Harlem; he had street knowledge. He spoke the gangs' language, and he was just what Y.D.I. needed. Occasionally I would drop by the bakery where he worked and try to enlist him for Y.D.I. I told him he'd be walking the streets reaching out to the kids. After we met a few times, he said he'd give it a try.

Anyone living on the streets can spot a phony fast, and Petey knew it. He was a cool Christian. He started talking to the kids at the candy store. There's one on every block. It's the hangout for penny ante action, toughs, drunks, pushers, and payoffs. He got to know the kids and told them what he'd done, where he'd been, and how it was better now. Kids listened and Petey listened to them.

We made the rounds greeting gang members hanging out on the streets. Kids were out to show "heart," or *machismo;* this raised their status. On the other end, the lowest rung in the ranks was a punk. Calling a kid a punk could get you a knife in the ribs.

There were times when just our presence stopped a potential rumble. At other times, we'd get word of a war and scramble to the scene, hoping to get there in time to throw the cold water of reason on gangs ready to ignite a "burn." We'd surround kids and go after the officers. "Shut up!" Petey once yelled at the president of the Hawks and the war counselor of the Red Wings, who were ready to "get it on" with each other. "Are you a bunch of punks or men? There's no use talking to punks." His question caught attention. Action froze. We held their attention while police circled in cars,

103

ready. I told the kids we'd get the police to split if the gangs broke it up. I huddled with a police sergeant and asked him to hang back. As we talked to the kids, the tension, tight as a tin can seal, eased as the boys were diverted from their rumble. It didn't always work this way. There would be a next time, but this temporary truce kept kids from being hurt or killed that night.

Sometimes we'd pile the gang presidents into the station wagon and get them out of the city to talk. Sometimes we'd drive them to my home in Tarrytown. I can imagine what the neighbors thought the first time they got a look at our guests. It always looked like a thousand clowns springing out of the station wagon. But the tough kids were as apprehensive as the neighbors; this wasn't their territory. We steered them into the basement to work out peace plans. Negotiations, persuasions, and resolutions often took hours. But if we got the magic words, "It's cool. It's off," that was well worth the time *and* many lives.

We weren't always out on the streets chasing down warring gangs. We had our quiet serious sessions at Y.D.I.'s storefront.

The kids in Harlem asked, "Are you for real?" We did our best to be. Sometimes it's simply the act of putting your hand on a kid's shoulder. That move says, "I know you are alive, you are someone." Maybe no one's ever done that to a kid before. Love and discipline were the two qualities missing in their young lives. Their family life was fragmented, and when there isn't enough to eat, or room to move, tenderness hardens, and discipline is too much trouble to dole out. At Y.D.I. I tried to supply large doses of both. By listening to a kid you can then start to work with words. Most of them had learned what they had to for their street life, we tried to show them what they needed for a whole life. We held informal Bible studies and exciting discussions about how Christ used people's lives today. The kids began to realize that there is a God who cares about them and that they are important to him. And they realized what it meant to accept Christ.

Of the first nine boys to come into Y.D.I., seven found a life very different from the one they were living. One became a prominent leader in the East Harlem community. Another went to work for Chase Manhattan Bank, and later became a junior executive. Still another one went to work for the United States Government. The others run the gamut from bakery foreman, industrial firm supervisor, to an electronics engineer. The seventh, after graduation from college, went to work with kids in the community, trying to teach them what he had learned.

Once in awhile a boy comes along who is a leader, a mover. Santy Lopez was a natural. He was known as the "good Lopez boy," and there were plenty of brothers to compare him with. This young boy was tough enough to take care of himself, but not one who took advantage of others. Santy, cheerful, involved, had just been voted the boy most likely to succeed at P.S. 117.

One evening at twilight, I pulled up in front of 2110 with a carload of boys. Santy was waiting outside with his brother Goldie. Santy called over the noise of the boys, who were becoming a ball of elbows trying to beat each other out of the car. "Mr. Jim, can we talk?" I waved the Lopez boys into the car and we drove off. "The gang on 109th Street, you know, they're after Goldie," said Santy. "They say they're going to burn him for holding out on drugs. But he doesn't have any."

Santy fed me the rest of the details he picked up about the planned shooting. It all sounded too familiar. I said I'd do my best to cool it and delivered the brothers to their apartment. I started back toward 2110, planning various strategies to negotiate peace. We had saved kids in the past by pulling together gang leaders for private meetings. I hoped I could work that tonight.

After dinner I was on my way back to 2110 when the call came on my car telephone. Santy was dead, shot in the back. I rushed to 117th and 3rd Avenue and found his blood still fresh on the sidewalk. An eerie calm prevailed. I walked down the street to the tenement where Santy's family lived. People gathered outside. I sensed the undercurrent of resentment and revenge as I cut through the crowd. I could hear his mother crying. Mrs. Lopez embraced me as I came in the door and just wouldn't let go. She cried all night. The headlines in the *New York Daily News* the following day told the story in brief words, "Slay Wrong Boy in Gang War." I had a sickening feeling of failure.

Boys weren't the only ones in trouble. Girls were linked to boys' gangs and some ran in packs of their own. We didn't have space in 2110 for a girls' program too. I was debating opening a second storefront for them when I met Mrs. Lyn Robinson at New Hyde Park Baptist Church where I was speaking. She cared about girls' problems and worried about their future. She volunteered to try to help.

In 1959 we opened a storefront on 108th Street that was manned by volunteers. The main attraction was the beauty shop, an instant hit. But it wasn't all lipstick and curlers. The girls still got into fights every bit as foul as the boys. Our volunteers were great, but not trained to handle the hard-core gang girls. I enlisted Vete Rust, who had done wonders with girls' gangs in Chicago, to help our girls. If they got out of hand, Vete would rush into the midst of fights and split them up. She'd help when they were pregnant, in trouble in court, and in any other way they needed her. We didn't have visions of reborn innocence but worked on changing their direction through showing Christ's example, and practical help.

106

We never produced instant angels. Some of our kids tried to dodge the law. Their fathers weren't around much and the mothers had obligations to other children so we'd play a big brother role in court. When a boy got into trouble, we would never give any information to the police without first asking if it was O.K. or saying, "Can I take you and stay with you while the police ask you about this?" The kid knew the police would probably find him anyway and usually agreed. Then, the only thing was to go with him and wait to put in a good word if we could. If it was a first offense, we'd try to get the kid released on probation to Y.D.I. No one else had ever done that for them. If trust was betrayed, and the boy went wrong again, then he was on his own with the police. We couldn't keep hauling him out of the courthouse so he could return to the scene of his crime and repeat it.

With more responsibility, we needed more staff to keep our efforts going. John Stanley joined in July 1961, as director of our city operations. He worked patiently at peeling off the layers of hostility and insecurity that make up the mentality of the troubled kids.

Y.D.I. drew some publicity in national magazines, and a Time-Life film team also got interested. They produced "Petey and Johnny," a documentary film about Y.D.I. with Petey Thomas as their star. It was later released on NBC TV. Petey, who had wanted to write, eventually left Y.D.I. to try his hand at that career. He devoted his time to writing a book about Spanish Harlem, *Down These Mean Streets,* that became a national best seller.

The streets calmed down quite a bit after our first years at 2110. I'll take some credit, but there was another force at work, one that took over the kids' lives. Drugs.

Kids had long been pumping marijuana into their systems and sniffing glue into their lungs, but hard drugs weren't on the streets much until the late fifties, and by the early sixties there was a drug epidemic. Drugs sapped gang power. Fewer kids swaggered off to fight. They did themselves in with heroin. Kids would skin pop, or drive the drug straight into their veins and vanish into a temporary, trouble-free neverland. They'd sit on steps and nod. A kid's head would bob down, down, until it hit his knee, bounce back up, back down, like a toy bird that perches on the edge of a glass and keeps reaching down for a drink of water.

Slowly the core of block social structure, the candy store where kids once met to plan wars, turned into an open drug connection point. Some kids, seeing a way to make real money, became dealers. Others started stealing to buy the stuff. The silence of the blocks grew sinister as more kids wasted themselves into oblivion.

We shifted our attention to include drug prevention, and later, rehabilitation.

In time we escaped the ingrown notion that cops, social workers, and teachers were in Harlem just for a job. The kids saw the cops bash heads and do-good social workers coming, and mostly going. Teachers had to cope with an educational system that often allowed students to go through high school without knowing how to read beyond the third-grade level. And the church—the church wasn't even in sight.

The vacated churches told the story with their signs, "No loitering." The church fled on the heels of the affluent congregations out to the suburbs. The once fashionable areas where the church had been active were now abandoned, deteriorating into ghettos. Nothing was left for the people who needed help the most. It's possible many of the vile conditions rampant in the inner city wouldn't have ever begun, or at least not multiplied so rapidly, if the church had stayed to help improve and rehabilitate those areas.

I checked around for a church that would open its doors to our kids. We were around for years before anyone gave a thought to inner-city kids. Calvary Baptist Church on West 57th Street invited us to join their Sunday school class. First thing on Sunday morning I would round up the kids. I'd go pounding on apartment doors, on car windows, in alleys. They wanted to go to Sunday school, but it was up to me to get them to the church on time. Asking them to meet me at eight o'clock at 2110 just didn't work. No one took the concept of time seriously. Time did not structure their lives; it was more like a paper clip, used to hold their days together.

When all were accounted for, our group of nine journeyed to midtown in my station wagon. That alone was an adventure. They had never ventured down to 57th Street alone, but united they stood, knowing from their street experience that there was strength in numbers.

Our boys were first assigned to the regular Sunday school; that didn't last long. These were pre-civil-rights days and when churchgoers got a look at our crowd, well behaved and well groomed, but scruffy in the best they had, many noses tilted upward. The church soon found us a room of our own where I took over the Sunday school class. Our numbers swelled. The station wagon was replaced by buses. We ended up with about a hundred kids, all types, from gang leaders to girls cradling babies. The church, perhaps embarrassed, perhaps simply overrun, finally asked us to use Steinway Hall, a building down the street, at their expense. The building belonged to the Steinway Piano Company and housed a concert hall plus a string of rooms for smaller recitals. There was room for all of us. Our kids had behaved themselves like cosmopolitan gentlemen at Calvary Baptist Church and continued to do so at

Steinway Hall, once they'd all had rides up and down the elevators. That kind of amusement was scarce in East Harlem.

Our trips to Steinway Hall showed me that the kids were ready for more outings. We'd all pile in the car and escape the confines of the block. I was our tour conductor as we investigated the Statue of Liberty and other famous monuments they never knew existed. We visited churches, parks, museums, airports, and beaches.

I also wanted the kids to see some open country with unpaved land where trees grew wild and people didn't. An obvious follow-up was camping out.

A friend of Y.D.I. had a place in Croton-on-Hudson, New York, with some land to roam around on and a small lake for swimming.

We readied ourselves to camp out with sleeping bags and tents from an army-navy surplus store. A church in Hawthorne, New Jersey, had a food drive. This enabled us to cook in tin cans on open fires. The only thing we weren't prepared for was an ambush by a blizzard of bloodthirsty mosquitoes. We took our lumps that weekend. From then on, we were fortified with insect repellent and had grand times at "Mosquito Gulch."

After two summers the property was sold out from under us. I hated to tell the kids, so I made a thorough search for a site we might, if God willed, eventually build a camp on. I called a commercial real estate man and detailed my ideal camp. He said he had one. It was an abandoned gravel pit in Glen Spey, New York. The entrance wasn't particularly glamorous, but the adjacent 60-acre lake and surrounding wooded area looked perfect. Timber for the gunboats of the Union Army was taken from this site. It was a 360-acre package, enough land for a real camp, not just a tame playground. But Y.D.I. couldn't cover the cost: $86,000. I asked for a three-month lease, with an option to buy. The three months were June, July, and August. For $500 we were set for the summer, if nothing else.

Camp got the kids into the outdoor world. Now I wanted to pop open the world of other ideas for them. I thought of Billy Graham instantly. He could open up Christ's message with his ability to talk in simple language.

Graham was deluged with demands on his time and it got tougher to keep in touch with him. I took a chance and called him to see if he could break out of his cramped schedule in order to take a side trip to Harlem. In addition to plain talk, he wasn't inhibited by the old cliché that if you work for Christ, you ought to be relegated to wearing shabby clothes. Graham says: "I represent the King of Kings, Lord of Lords, why shouldn't I look sharp?" When he came to 2110 to talk to the boys, walk the streets with them, and visit their families he led many to change their lives for Christ.

His Y.D.I. fan club grew even stronger when his wife, Ruth, wrote and offered us a soda fountain that her husband had been given for a TV appearance. We had just the place for it in our snack bar: the vacant area where the Coke machine used to be. Our kids, schooled in getting something for nothing, knew exactly how to coax Cokes out without money. When it came time to collect the proceeds from the coin box the distributor found it, as well as the Coke bottles, empty. The kids took over their new soda fountain and scooped up some of the wildest ice cream concoctions known to man.

Because Billy Graham made such an impact upon the boys, I decided that I'd try to get other prominent men to talk to the kids. They could share their witness and philosophies of life. I wanted to organize a regular series of evenings. I invited people with varied backgrounds and talents, then reserved a room at Steinway Hall. We attracted quite an array of speakers.

Some of the speakers were: our own police captain Conrad Jensen; Jerome Hines of the Metropolitan Opera Company; the late Roger Hull, president of Mutual of New York; and George Champion, president of Chase Manhattan Bank. They were all terrific and George Champion, among others, was to become a special man in my life, and Y.D.I.'s.

I had met Champion at Billy Graham's New York crusade in 1957. Champion and Roger Hull served as co-chairmen. Roger Hull was the M.C. while Champion worked behind-the-scenes to make the crusade a success. Even before we met, friends had suggested I contact Champion about helping, but I was hesitant about ringing strange doorbells. We met again at a small gathering of the Protestant Council of New York. Alice and I were seated with the Champions during dinner. He asked about my work and I told him briefly of Y.D.I. I didn't see him again until he arrived to speak at Steinway Hall.

I'm amazed that George Champion accepted my invitation to talk to the boys at Steinway Hall, now that I know what a busy night it was for him. He did a brilliant job of giving his city audience a verbal portrait of his early life as a farmboy in Illinois and his climb to the heights of the New York financial community.

His delivery was in the Will Rogers tradition and the kids loved it. I found out as he was leaving that he saved time for Y.D.I. on the same night as the grand opening of Chase Manhattan Plaza, headquarters for one of the world's largest banks. While he spoke, former governor and presidential candidate Tom Dewey was waiting down in the limousine to continue on, late, to the bank's ceremony.

A few months later word got to me at 2110 that Y.D.I. was being investigated. A judge I had worked with in family court reported that people had questioned her about us. My school buddies, Flax, Gersh, and Captain Jensen at the police department told me someone had checked with them, too.

Evidently they all said the right things. Late one night, soon after I had learned of this unidentified interested party, there was a knock at 2110. I checked the television screen but didn't recognize the man until he told me who, was on the intercom. It was George Champion whom I hadn't seen since he spoke at Steinway Hall. He was on his way back from a trip to Washington, D.C., and had stopped by to chat. He questioned me at length about Y.D.I.'s programs. He had met many of the kids at Steinway Hall, now he was on their own turf. He asked what our greatest need was. I answered, "A camp." I told him we had found a beautiful site with 360 acres that we had leased for the summer. "How much?" came his next question. "The asking price is $86,000 for the property and it'll take about another million to complete it." Champion thought it over for a few minutes, then said, "I promise to cover you on the purchase price." He added, "Then we'll see what we can do about the rest." As we talked I figured out the riddle of who had conducted the investigation of Y.D.I. From that point on, Champion took responsibility for raising money to purchase the camp.

Champion asked to come on the board of directors in order to establish an official tie with Y.D.I. for reasons having to do with fund-raising. Any other group would have voted him in in thirty seconds, but I wondered if he would ever belong to Y.D.I.'s board. They had to get over their hang-ups about admitting Champion. The members were worried that Champion's views of the Christian faith might not coincide with

113

theirs. It took a glowing recommendation of Champion from Billy Graham to convince the board, two months later, to vote him on. It was just as difficult to add two other board members. Champion asked for John B. M. Place, a former vice president of Chase Manhattan Bank, now president of Anaconda; and Donald L. Wallace, an attorney, to handle the financial responsibilities. Apprehension vanished when the charter members saw how dedicated the new members were.

Champion's arena was the financial community. He invited friends, eight or ten at a time, to luncheons held in the Chase Manhattan Bank's dining room. I was to give an informal talk about what I was doing in Harlem. The first meeting I looked around in awe at the tycoons, wondering what I was doing there with presidents of companies, managers of industry. I'd heard about people like them and knew some of their names, but hardly believed I'd be sitting down to lunch with them.

That was especially true of Tom Dewey. I remembered him waving at a crowd from his car during his presidential campaign in Los Angeles. I was in that crowd of onlookers.

However, I relaxed once I realized that, though their suits might be better tailored than most, these were not only interesting but interested men. Many of them were more than politely generous toward Y.D.I. Ten- and fifteen-thousand-dollar allotments weren't uncommon. But the checks that startled me the most were of modest amounts when they came in from a friend of Champion's, President Dwight D. Eisenhower.

13

Chapter

Our camp building fund grew as George Champion did an excellent job of bringing support to Y.D.I. Champion wisely reasoned that the money we received from his associates were one-time gifts and Y.D.I. should not be dependent on them. Therefore, these sums were allocated for capital expenses, not operational costs. To get the camp moving I had to do my part too.

That put me back on the road fund-raising, traveling, and speaking about Y.D.I.

I've never had a lot of spare time and I resented the days I lost driving, days I could have been with the kids. I didn't have any hours left to make up the time. I was getting by nicely on four or five hours sleep, but I did need those. The only place I could hope to save any time was on transportation. I toyed with the thought of buying a small airplane. It could be amortized as a business expense and supported with travel expenses given me by the various groups. More to the point, I could save hundreds of hours. My first step was to learn to fly, and to see if I liked it. I discovered that I loved flying. In a few months I was a licensed pilot. I bought a single engine Piper Cherokee. If it turned out that the plane didn't work to ease my traveling woes, I could sell it and hit the highways again. That plane cut hours off travel time, and besides, it was fun. I soon traded in the single for a twin engine that was larger and, therefore, safer for night flying and longer trips.

After I started flying to meetings, a friend in Tarrytown mentioned that a neighbor, Paul Wheatley, enjoyed flying and might be interested in being a co-pilot just for the ride. I had met him once before in his office. He was a notary and had notarized some business papers for Y.D.I. I didn't like hopping around alone, especially on night flights, so I called him to see if he'd like to take some trips. I don't think then he knew what he was getting into. My schedule would be as busy as any airline's, in order to speak at as many places as possible each trip. Unfortunately, they weren't often in the same part of the country.

"There never was anything that could be called a normal routine schedule," sighs Wheatley. "In one year we made over one hundred different stops. They were mostly sandwiched in between Friday and Sunday nights, although we'd make a few midweek trips. Luckily, we both enjoyed flying. With this kind of traveling, getting there is almost all the fun, the rest of the time it is so rushed. When we would arrive, I'd play the part of advance man and make sure things were set up. If Jim was using electronics, I'd check to see if there were outlets and see that the equipment was set up correctly.

"I also got us both out of a lot of tea and cookie sessions. It's not that there's anything wrong with tea and cookies, but after having buzzed around in the air for hours and then speaking and participating in a discussion period afterwards, even Jim was tired. I'd say just loud enough for everyone to overhear, 'Jim, I

*know you don't want to, but we've got to go. The weather in the
south looks like it's getting worse. If we don't leave within the
next fifteen minutes, we won't be able to get into the airport.' And,
as often as not, he would have another meeting scheduled two
hours later two hundred miles away.*

*"The only kinks I never straightened out in all our air travels
were the wrinkles in Jim's suits. He couldn't arrive rumpled, so
he'd usually have to bring along a second suit and change at the
motel. On one trip, he was scheduled to talk to a small group
meeting in a Chinese restaurant in Los Angeles, just minutes after
we landed. There wasn't time for him to stop and change. At the
restaurant, I explained our situation thoroughly to the owner and
asked to borrow a room for a few moments. But after all my
frantic babbling, I realized he didn't understand English. I didn't
understand Chinese. Sign language didn't work either. We ended
up commandeering the men's room for ten minutes. I stood watch
and turned away customers who, like the owner, were totally
bewildered."*

As our fund-raising efforts bore fruits, I was delighted to tell the real estate man that giving us the summer
lease with option to buy was a gamble that had paid off.
The day we nailed down the purchase I was outside my
house in Tarrytown collecting the mail and called to
my neighbor, "Hey, Larry, we got it!"

"What's that, Jim?" he answered.

"We got our camp for the kids. We just bought the
land."

"Great, where is it?"

Glen Spey, New York. It's a little . . ."

Larry cut me short and led me into his house, "I
want you to meet Miller Fagley from Glen Spey, New
York."

I was surprised anyone had heard of the town, let
alone known someone from it.

I was introduced to Fagley who said he was a contractor.

"Do you build houses?" I asked.

117

"Yes."

"Can you build a camp?"

Our conversation was racing rapidly into a business deal until I slowed it down by saying, "I don't have the money to build yet, but we will soon." We set a meeting date in Glen Spey.

At the appointed hour I went to meet Miller Fagley. He was there waiting, a trim, thoughtful man, puffing on his pipe. We sat by the side of the country road and I talked about what I wanted for the kids. Then we got into buildings and what the camp would need. From our first meeting, we've been able to communicate easily with each other, never faltering because one misunderstood the other's words. The opposite was true of the architect I hired to draw up my plans. I never could get through to him what I wanted.

A little working time with Miller showed me that he was an extraordinary man, a perfectionist in everything he did. I decided we'd take on the designs for the buildings ourselves and forget the architect. We scratched out sketches in the sand on the bank of the lake. There seemed to be an appropriate spot for every building we wanted to place; as if the land was mapped out, waiting for us. Perhaps Miller did more formal outlines after our sand sketching, but I seldom saw him with a blueprint. There wasn't much at first. He cleared and filled the gravel pit, put in underground electricity, and sunk a well.

14

Chapter

Our empty acreage became Camp Y.D.I. and the lake was named Lake Champion in honor of George Champion. It was exhilarating to be there that first summer, knowing that the open fires would be replaced by a dining hall, and the tents by real cabins. Best of all, it was a permanent camp and all ours.

At our dedication ceremony an air of tranquility reigned during the prayer. The kids quieted, closed their eyes, and bowed their heads for this special time. Reveling in the promise of the moment, I looked up to get a visual imprint of all those serene faces. My reverie was abruptly interrupted by a young girl, stark naked, taking advantage of the closed eyes, changing out of her bathing suit into dry clothes.

The site for the director's cabin got a name when George Champion paid his first visit. Everything was going perfectly for Champion's look at the camp; it sparkled and the food was good. I hoped that he would like what he had worked so hard to make possible. After lunch I took him for a walk. We headed down the knoll toward the lake. A thunderstorm caught us halfway there. We had no warning, no shelter and got soaked clear through to our socks. Sheepishly, I began to apologize for marching him out into a rainstorm when a brilliant rainbow divided the sky. Champion turned and said, "That rainbow is one of the most beautiful moments in my life. It's all the proof I need that the camp is what it should be." Later we named the director's cabin Rainbow's End. Later, the camp, as well as the lake, was named after George Champion, over his loud objections. Whether he would admit it or not, he, more than anyone, is responsible for Camp Champion.

In the early days I was camp director and cook. The kitchen was a large open barbecue pit to the left of the lake. Talk about hungry mouths to feed. Those kids were starving all the time. One day at lunch time I was out there flipping hamburger patties on the grill when a visitor strolled over. I'm usually hospitable, but in the middle of cooking the kids' lunch, I didn't dare take time out to be polite and burn the food. The guy saw my dilemma, pitched in and shared my chef's duty.

When the food was doled out, my fellow cook got a hamburger for his efforts. Then we got around to formal introductions. He was Alan Betts, a friend of George Champion, up from New York and the Astor Foundation. And I had put him to work turning meat patties!

I gave him a thorough tour of the camp, pointing out the places we planned to build. A week later I got a call from Betts. He said he liked the way we were running the camp, the economical and practical methods we used, then offered us $300,000. I didn't say no, but after I started adding up our budget, I figured we weren't ready for $300,000. I called back and asked

Betts for $150,000 instead. He couldn't believe I would refuse half the money; no one had ever done that. But he did give us the $150,000. I guess I still thought the remaining half was marked for us because I called Betts about a year later and asked for the rest of "our $300,000." He chuckled. We got it.

Contributions, large and small, from people across the country have made Camp Champion a success. When Mark O. Hatfield, governor of Oregon, came east he paid Y.D.I. a visit. I couldn't resist wondering aloud, why couldn't a governor of a state that boasted the largest lumber industry come up with some lumber for our camp buildings. "That's a good question," replied Hatfield. I got my real answer a few weeks later. A man called, mentioned Hatfield's name and said, "I understand you need some lumber. Do you have any idea how much material you'll need?" I just happened to have a list.

Sometimes donations turned out to be more trouble than they were worth, like our Greyhound buses. We finagled Greyhound into lending us buses to get our kids around. I've never been sure if that was a blessing or a curse because they broke down so often. We weren't experienced bus drivers and didn't know when, or how many times per trip, we'd hear that clicking sound that meant we were stuck, or soon would be. Depending on how sick the bus was and how slick a mechanic we could turn up, a trip normally taking two hours could take as many as five or six. We've since taken Greyhound's advice; we leave the driving to them.

Over the years the camp has grown up to be a combination of manicured manor and natural wilderness, sculpted by Miller's fine hand.

A large velvet lawn embroidered with butterfly-bright flowers carpets the entrance. To the left, a small pond reflects the clear sky. To the right, like a gem in

121

a perfect setting, is the chapel, with large windows curtained by the lace of leafy trees and ferns.

To the lower right in the farmland, complete with a barn, there is a decorative donkey or two for city kids who've never seen one and Meadowmaid, a cow, to prove that milk doesn't come in cartons. Up the road into the main camp there is an athletic field and administration building.

The dining hall, the first structure we built, sits atop a grassy knoll that glides down into the 60-acre lake. The kitchen inside is first rate. There are five oversize ovens, long sinks, giant-size equipment and supplies, enough to feed an army. The current chef, Henry Bosch, has had practice. He was General George Patton's personal chef.

The cabins are set up in clusters of villages tucked into the woods out of sight of the lake. The kids aren't exactly roughing it. Each camper has a bed. The counselor's bed is walled off in a closet-size cubby, and there's a bathhouse in each village.

Around the lake and on the trails, nothing has been touched. Trees filter the sun onto moss covered logs and lush wild ferns. The sounds are of birds, fish, and the winds sweeping through branches. And, of course, campers.

There are those who say the camp is too plush. But these kids are tossed secondhand clothes and live in overpopulated, ill equipped quarters. That's all they know. At camp they get clean cabins, clean bathrooms, plus regular meals which provide real nourishment and an example of clean living. But it's more than that!

Miller re-created an early New England covered bridge to connect the village to the main camp. The wood was first used in a neighbor's barn in 1790. The kids needed a raft to float on the lake; Miller built the U.S.S. *Tom Sawyer*. Even the railings around the porches are extraordinary, silhouettes of arrows that point up toward heaven. Once I asked him why. He replied, "Isn't that what this is all about?"

It took Miller awhile to decide to become resident manager after he put up the buildings. He had a young daughter, Kathy, and was a bit nervous about her being around all those city boys. And, of course, it meant that his life would be lived at the camp, not in town. We had a talk. "Miller, you don't have to live here at camp, but I would like you to design a nice home with all the facilities you'd want for a resident manager—whoever that may be." "O.K." he agreed. "Another thing, I know you haven't decided if you'll live here or not, but I would like the house to be all ready by Christmas. I want to be sure there's a fireplace, good kitchen, and comfortable rooms; so just go to it." He built a finely detailed, comfortable house. After the house was completed, I asked, "How about moving your family in for Christmas?" He did.

The community thought it was great to have a camp for poor kids from the city, but wished it was somewhere else. Some were scared. One woman refused to use the road that passed in front of camp. She circled all the way around, and that was more than just a few miles out of her way. Others were nasty. During early construction our Lake Champion sign was torn down. In its place, "This way to the tax free nigger camp." It only represented the views of a few, but it sure made a lot of people feel bad. The summer folks weren't any more receptive. We imported what they came all the way out of the city to get away from. They resented us. So we started to work to win them over.

The most influential man we had was Miller Fagley. Glen Spey was his town. He became our spokesman. People, mad about our bussing kids to their beautiful countryside, were skeptical about listening even to

Miller. But eventually, he and a local insurance man invited some townspeople to dinner as Y.D.I.'s guests. After dinner, we got down to business. I told them I had heard the rumors that an ex-gangster opened some sort of camp for a crowd of city thugs. I told them it wasn't as bad as it sounded. I went over my life story, then talked about Y.D.I. and the kids, explaining what we were doing. I assured the group that they wouldn't see kids running wild through town. We made sure they stayed on the camp grounds. We had 360 acres, and that was enough room to run. I didn't get any rousing ovations, but the community people calmed down enough to take a wait-and-see attitude, rather than trying to kick us out.

We did our best to be responsible to the community. The camp is tax exempt, but we made contributions to the fire department and highway fund equivalent to the taxes we otherwise would have paid. We slowly earned Glen Spey's approval. Eventually the residents grew easy with us as neighbors.

With local relations established, we also had to learn how to live with ourselves. You can take kids out of the city, but you've got to remember who they are and take control.

Once, before we knew what we were dealing with, we parked the bus outside a department store. The kids got off to take a look around while the bus was getting fixed. We were happy to finally get going up to camp. Only then, after the campers and their luggage were out, did we discover how the kids amused themselves during our recess for repairs. The bus was full of merchandise they had lifted from the store. We went back to return the goods and made sure that never happened again.

Young people know what they're capable of doing, and they'll lay out test after test to see who's in charge.

You have to pass, or it's chaos. If necessary, we ladle out large doses of discipline, and the camp programs have always been tightly structured. Sessions range from remedial tutoring in reading and math, Bible studies, to waterfront and pioneer activities.

"If we turned the camp over to the campers, they would probably start the first session off by burning down a village," sighs Alec Rowland, executive director of Y.D.I. Alec took his turn running Camp Champion with his wife, Rita. These two twenty-five-year-olds sailed through a smooth summer program their first year out.

One of our original plans was to have the camp serve as a feeder program for city work. There is no charge, except a five-dollar transportation fee, so the kids will feel committed enough to show up for the bus. This lets in a lot of kids we wouldn't otherwise get and Rowland put it well. "Camp may be the only shot we get at the kids. So we work hard."

Though the camp is definitely domesticated, rural living is still a struggle for these young people who call New York's toughest square mile home. The wildest life that comes into the camp are a few grain-fed deer, as docile as puppy dogs, and some adventurous chipmunks.

The kids may have been as far into the outdoors as Central Park. They have to be taught how to handle themselves, how to play games. They grew up with stick ball in the street, but a baseball diamond is new. Most have to be taught how to swim. At first, they may not want any part of these new activities, but our rule is, participate! After they get their feet wet in a new sport and build some confidence, they have a great time.

"I first heard about Camp Champion ten years ago," remembers veteran counselor, Lillian Rivera. She started as a camper when, "My friends told me that it was a great place and that you

125

didn't have to pay anything to go. I've been coming to camp for ten years, first as a camper, then as a counselor. I can see now that it takes kids time to get over being scared of things, the way I was at first. Two of my girls went on a canoe trip. They didn't want to at first, but I talked to them awhile in our cabin. They finally decided to go, and they loved it.

"Working at camp helps my work in the city during the winter. When I see the kids I know who they are. I've been swimming with them and have eaten meals with them. We have experiences to build a relationship on. And it's good for them, and me, to get out of the city."

We encourage wilderness hikes to let them see areas where man hasn't manufactured the landscape. The hikers do well until the sun sinks; then the darkness fires their incredibly rich imaginations. Every sound becomes a grizzly bear, or maybe a wolf. Twigs turn into snakes. One moonless night, the two counselors in charge hung back from their group of hikers to decide which trail to follow back to camp. The boys walked on, chattering. Suddenly, they realized they were alone. "Where are we?" "How will we ever get back to camp?" "What will we do?" "What was that noise?" The counselors, having settled the route, had almost caught up with the boys when they heard their confusion and decided to see what the kids would do on their own. The campers' voices grew shrill until one boy looked up and said "Let's pray." The counselors beamed. The kids decided a boy named Felix would say the prayer. He tried to duck, then went ahead: "Please God, help us out of this darkness. Lead us, your lost children, back to camp safely. Amen." Each boy added his amen. Silence. Then, after a golden moment, the silence was shattered by another voice, "O.K. now what the ——— we do?"

126

15

Chapter

It's disheartening, with all we tried to do, to see the youth coming back from the mountains having to face reality again, with real rats, not chipmunks.

We were attentive to outside proposals of how to better the boys' ability to pull themselves out of their cracked plaster world. One try was Operation Springboard, which we co-founded with Captain Jensen when he retired from the police force. Jensen wanted to teach the kids woodworking. Expanding the boys' skills was a good idea, but it was born to fail, and sadly, it affected our relationship. Even away from the force, it was tough for Jensen to forget he was a cop. It was tougher for the kids. During the short time we ran Operation Springboard we produced some furniture, but the kids and Jensen couldn't manufacture any real rapport between them.

With the establishment of Operation Springboard, the bond between Jensen and me began to break. Jensen, who had helped Y.D.I. immeasurably when I first arrived in Harlem, now began tearing it down, complaining about the way it was run. Nothing was quite right for him. In the midst of a Christian organization, infighting crept in. Jensen's temper flared if we didn't have a half hour of prayer before every staff meeting. I countered that I believed in prayer, but not as ritual to satisfy others; that was meaningless. Operation Springboard's closing set him off on a final round of petty gripes about camp and office supply costs. Then he resigned.

Jensen's leaving was followed by another bittersweet chapter in Y.D.I. history. In January 1963 tragedy sprang swiftly as a coiled snake, poisoning a party of innocents and striking one down. Lou Marsh, a city youth board member, spotted four of our boys, ex-gang-leader Tony Blondet, James Griffin, Steve Naranjo, and Teddy Shepherd, walking down Second Avenue at 112th Street. Marsh tried to stop them. Apparently he wanted to talk them out of what he thought was a fight in the making. The only fight in sight was stirred up by Marsh's intervention. The boys contended he had no authority over them. An argument followed, then grew when Marsh raised his fists, as though to fight. One of the boys pushed him to one side. A moment later Marsh's body became rigid and he fell backward, cracking his skull on the sidewalk. He never regained consciousness and died two days later.

News sources enlarged the story of the youth worker struck down by hoodlums and swayed public sentiment in sympathy for the dead Lou Marsh.

Believing there was more to the story, we talked to the boys and defended them when they were tried for manslaughter in the court and in the newspapers.

The opposition painted as bleak a picture of the boys as they could conjure up. They dragged out the juicy parts of my past, hoping to smear Y.D.I. because I had been jailed. The trial brought out new facts that we thought would clear our boys. Shepherd and the others weren't guilty of playing dirty and hurting Marsh when he was down, as the newspaper stories had it. Marsh was an epileptic. He had been caught up in a grand mal seizure at the moment he raised his fists.

At the end of the proceedings, the judge instructed the jury that if they determined the action of the boys in any way caused the grand mal seizure—through verbal threats, excitement of a possible impending fight—then they were as responsible for his death as if they had physically beaten him.

All four were judged guilty through no wrong act of their own and sent to jail for manslaughter.

We kept in touch with them in jail. Here's a letter Tony Blondet wrote to Y.D.I.'s John Stanley from prison:

Dear John:

It remains my prayer that the Lord may choose to safeguard you and all dear to you, and that the receipt of this message may find you in good spirits.

In the time passed between letters your friend became the holder of a Regent's diploma. Yes, passing the Spanish Regents' exam gave me enough credits for a diploma. The mark was 92, which results in my having an 88 average.

And, changing the subject to you, how are things down yonder? In your last letter you confirmed the tragic news about Bat. I hope that you will be able to reach some of the others down there with Christ's message before confirmation of such grim tidings becomes necessary for them also. Of course, from experience this writer knows how set against salvation many, especially young people, seem to be. But, I am praying that the truth you bring in Christ's name will prevail over their reticence.

Again, I must confirm your suspicions of my ever-growing interest in Christ. It is a source of great comfort and strength to have found someone of whose love there can be no doubt. His guidance has become a necessary part of my life and through the Lord I have come to know myself as never before.

It has been over a year, but I still remember the letter Jim wrote us after the trial, in which he admonished us to strengthen our bodies and minds, but most of all to strengthen our newly formed bonds with Christ.

So praying that your success in lodging in open hearts the word of Christ is many times multiplied,

My love to everyone at the club.

Your friend, Antonio.
July 6, 1965.

Today Tony explains his feeling about the trial:
"I felt bad 'cause something we did caused Marsh to lose his life. We didn't really hurt him, but it still happened. If we'd wanted to hurt him, we would have, and there would have been no doubt we meant to. I didn't get too bitter because I know if this hadn't happened I would have been on drugs or in some kind of fight because of the life I was still a part of.

"Steve Naranjo lives in the same project today, going to school under the Higher Education Opportunity Program. Teddy Shepherd died of an overdose. Ironically, he had just come around and started working, just getting straight with himself. I haven't heard from James Griffin for a couple of years. Last time I saw him he was big and fat, not doing much good or bad."

The boys and I weren't the only ones tumbling on the legal trampoline that year. Mickey Cohen managed to get himself turned upside down in court for writing and overselling a book.

After he had been released from his first three-year jail term, I suggested he write a book of memoirs. He thought it a terrific idea, and worked on it every morning for months. What he didn't tell me was as soon as he had structured an outline, he showed it to friends and sold them rights to his forthcoming book—at least 150 percent of it. He scraped together over a million dollars by dragging around his unfinished manuscript. The ever ready IRS hounded Cohen and found out about his extraordinary money-finding powers. He explains the background:

"My problem came when Police Chief Parker, an old enemy of mine, came into power in Los Angeles. He went to Washington and got Attorney General Kennedy's ear. Parker was out to get me and told Kennedy that if the federal government didn't go after me, there was no way to convict me. He pushed it and pushed it."

Cohen got picked up for tax evasion. His defense was that the money was loaned, therefore, not taxable income. The IRS countered that Cohen was a con artist and the money he collected was fruit of his labor as a con man, in other words, income.

Cohen went back to prison, this time for fifteen years, one of the harshest sentences ever passed against an individual for tax shenanigans.

16 Chapter

Y.D.I.'s only office was a very small one back in Grants Pass, Oregon, until the summer of 1959 when we opened a one room office on the second floor of the Lyceum Building in Tarrytown.

At first I'd just step in for a few hours, but as the years passed and Y.D.I. grew, the paperwork increased and sapped my time from city work. To get Y.D.I. and me out from under a paper avalanche I took courses in computer programming to try and unload the paperwork onto a computer.

My math and science background made it easy to learn, even fun. I worked many mornings from 3:00 A. M. to program the computer. It was worth it. I fed Y.D.I.'s paperwork into the computer to store records, mailing lists, and reports for auditors. I cut down on time and clerical help. Betty Craig, two other typists, and one computer handled the work.

In spite of the long hours I was able to keep some

time aside for my family and made sure we got into Manhattan for dinner or a show once a month.

In the summers we all went to camp. Our "cabin," really a house at Rainbow's End, was close to the main camp yet separate enough to allow us periods of privacy. Madeline, Dennis, Steve, and Roger were growing up; however, Madeline was having trouble.

Up to this point she had been a model child and an honor student. Out of the blue Alice and I received a note from Madeline's junior high school teacher. It told us Madeline was misbehaving. She tossed pennies all over the classroom.

It was an odd thing for Madeline to do. Surrounded by rough and tumble brothers she was a well-behaved, quiet child. The note was momentarily upsetting. In spite of our concern we thought it was an isolated outburst.

Then Madeline's principal sent a second note just before her graduation from junior high. I went in to talk with him. He asked us to keep her home for the remaining two weeks of school. Madeline had sent the teacher a message saying she was going to kill her.

Thinking that Madeline was doing this for attention, we honored the teacher's request and kept Madeline home with the understanding she would be graduated in June.

That summer she went with us to New Orleans where I had a speaking engagement. She was sullen, but nothing strange happened. In the fall, she started high school.

"When the high school teacher phoned, we knew Madeline's troubles were not over," recalls Alice. "Again she had threatened to kill a teacher.

"The school psychologist suggested she be given tests to determine her problem. Jim and I took her for testing and diagnosis. The report brought a real shock to both of us. She was diagnosed

schizophrenic with homicidal and suicidal tendencies. They rec-
ommended immediate hospitalization. I was not prepared for this
and it was a long time before I really believed she might follow
up on what I had taken to be a harmless threat."

One psychiatrist thought she might be able to lead a relatively normal life outside the hospital. We arranged for treatment twice a week and she lived at home. For a period of four months she seemed to improve. Then came the report that she set a fire in the girls' bathroom at school. The same day, Alice found a torn note in Madeline's bedroom wastebasket. She had written it the night before, after baby-sitting at a neighbor's. "I almost killed the baby last night" read the message on the reconstructed bits of paper. Our decision was made for us.

It's frustrating to attempt to ferret out a reason for something like Madeline's illness when all we have is a finite view of God's universe. God gave man free choice so the world wouldn't be populated by programmed robots. If God took total authority, we would have heaven on earth. We don't, and sometimes it hurts.

After nine years of heartbreak and disappointment, Madeline appears to be improving. She is not hospitalized at this time.

17

Chapter

Urban renewal hit in the late 1960s when Harlem got a facelift at 112th-115th streets. High-rise, low-income apartment buildings replaced aged brownstones. But this did nothing to nourish hope-starved residents who had neither jobs, nor what I felt was their greatest need, education. As Y.D.I. expanded my dreams grew with it. We could truly serve the community if we would tuck our club room under one umbrella with an academically accredited school, including medical and dental facilities.

At the same time my interest began to rise to the challenge of creating a complete center. Our building at 2110 was about to crumble from neglect. The landlord turned a deaf ear to our continual pleas for repairs. We turned on the pressure. I contacted the city and got the landlord ordered to fix the decaying building. He never came near it. What I succeeded in doing is something I hadn't planned; the building was condemned by the city. In September, we learned we had to the end of November to vacate. While looking for a new place, I saw one drab building after another until I found a flower in the desert, the Manhattan School of Music on 105th Street. It was a series of three interconnecting buildings. The main structure was an elevated building, five stories high with a gym and stage on the lower floor. There were two adjoining buildings, each three stories high.

The former tenants had recently moved to a new home. The building was up for grabs at $1,175,000. I set out like a politician after the vote to get the school. The pace at the office, never dull, was cranked up to top speed. We put together a brochure as fast as a newspaper's front page. Then we managed to piece together film clips about our work into a pretty good film illustrating our hopes and dreams. Time was short, so we concentrated our efforts. I phoned twelve couples from all parts of the United States who were major contributors to Y.D.I. and asked them to come east. We took them to Camp Champion. After a day of relaxation in the woods, where changing leaves flashed vibrant yellows and reds and the weather was clear and crisp against the color, we showed our film and told our guests of our dilemma at Hell Gate. We asked that they gather people together in their area for me to come talk to. Tom Cummings of the Cummings Sign Company in Nashville, Tennessee, loaned us his Lear jet. If Paul Wheatley thought my schedule was wild before, that was nothing compared to this race against a Thanksgiving deadline.

After completing a frenzied speaking circuit, I headed home to a big letdown. The beginning of the campaign was a bust. Nickels trickled in. Thanksgiving was near and so was our end-of-the-month eviction day. I was concerned about where we would move. By the middle of the month the flow of contributions started to strengthen into a real stream and then into a gush that pushed us over our goal, appropriately, by Thanksgiving Day.

We called the new acquisition Crossroads High School. The emphasis was on small classroom study so students would get the intense training they needed. The ratio of students to teacher was six to one, instead of the public school's thirty-five or forty-five to one. We intended to expand as our first students advanced to upper grades.

With our budget carefully allocated, we were ready for business. I went to work recruiting the best staff available by anyone's standards. I wanted them to be racially mixed and innovative. Our principal was a West Indian with a doctoral degree from Columbia. Bob Santilli, a trained chemist with an M.A. in theology from Princeton came to work with us. And so the posts filled up. The state of New York granted full accreditation. This time when Y.D.I. opened, we got 120 kids immediately.

I relaxed when we started school in September, 1970. We were grateful to all the people around the country who had sent in contributions and who were praying with us that our school would go.

By early November, the figures went sour on the operational end. Miraculously we had raised the money to buy the building but we couldn't accelerate the cash flow to meet the steady rise in daily costs.

At the end of November, 1970, I gave my first formal appeal to "stop spending." It wasn't the last. I nattered, I nagged, I pleaded, I ordered that spending be slowed down. No one listened. While I attempted to trim salaries and personnel, the principal was out hiring people. Then he ordered a $20,000 language laboratory. With that, we went under. After we recovered from the shock, I planned to start again on a shoestring operation. I didn't have a chance. I repeated what I had been yelling, "We don't have money, the purse is empty."

I met with our staff and laid out the reasons why the school's doors had to be shut. I answered their barrage of questions as best I could, and agreed to keep the school open until the end of the term in June. They weren't satisfied and bedlam broke loose.

It got much worse later when I met with the parents and students, about 200 of them. We met in the school cafeteria on the fifth floor. They were joined by an agitated staff, the principal leading the pack. It appeared to be a division between a few whites and many of the minority groups. These people had seen so many things just beyond their reach, and right then they were venting years of pent-up frustration.

Betty Craig and Paul Wheatley joined me in this meeting. I got a verbal knife stuck in my back and real spit in my face. At one point, when the sparks seemed to ignite a real inferno, I feared more for Betty and Paul's lives than I did for my own.

In the midst of the noisy din one message continually came through: "The school is the greatest thing that has happened to us and to the community, you can't take it away." They saw me as a big white man, somehow hanging from above and handing down crumbs. So quickly they forgot about our love, our caring through the years, the many who had been reached, the lives that had been changed. At last the turmoil was over, and Betty, Paul, and I got out safely.

Another blow came the day school closed; a lawsuit was leveled against Crossroads High School. Actually, it was two suits; one on part of the staff, and the other a class action suit representing the people of the community. They hired a storefront lawyer who tried for 1 million dollars. The suit claimed Y.D.I. funds had been improperly diverted from the school. They demanded we be stopped from selling the building and that the school be continued for a minimum of three more years, even though I had explained in great detail that we were broke.

Our case went to the Supreme Court of the State of New York. It cost Y.D.I. $10,000 in legal fees before the court granted a ruling in our favor. The court stated, "While the failure of the school to continue is regrettable, especially in view of the professed goals and aspirations of all concerned, financial necessity makes few compromises with idealism," and ruled, "This court cannot conclude on the basis of the papers before it that the closing of the school was a result of anything other than economic necessity." We received that news the day before Christmas, but it didn't make me feel much better about the school. For the first time since those formative days, I was tempted to quit. Now everything I had gotten started was going against me. Not one person said a thank you for the years I'd poured out to make the community grow and develop, or even for starting the school. I wanted to walk away. Yet, I felt I had a commitment to God to finish the program, and we had a bunch of kids with nowhere to go.

We had to sell the building, but before we were out some vandals had a party. The principal's office, one of the nicest, was methodically wrecked, ripped, and coated with glue. I was caught between being furious and crushed. It took some concentration before I was able or willing to focus on the Bible verse: "For what glory is it, if, when ye be buffeted for your faults, ye shall take it patiently? but if, when ye do well, and suffer for it, ye take it patiently, this is acceptable with God" (1 Peter 2:20).

The Board of Education took an interest in our

concept and bought the building to continue a similar program. The community cooled down.

Y.D.I. bounced back on a reduced program at 222 East 105th Street, under the direction of Bob Santilli, one of the few staff members from the school to stay with us. *"Though our space has been cut back, recreation and sports programs still run all the time. That's the method we use in offering them another way of living within the Christian dimension,"* says Santilli. *"We're street oriented and leave ourselves available to counteract the insecurity of street living. We try to show a new way of life, not cover old sores with token BandAids."*

To accomplish this, there are tandem programs, Crossroads Center and Crossroads House.

Crossroads Center runs two programs—separate care for the younger ones five through twelve and the traditional program for kids eighteen and over. The center thrives on vital chaos created by these youth.

"Bible studies!" a voice screams loud enough for the entire neighborhood to hear. There follows what seems to be the sound effects of a cattle stampede for a western movie as the little ones scramble upstairs en masse. They listen to stories and sing songs about the Lord. This gives other counselors time to clean up the kitchen after the kids baked banana bread. In the downstairs office, Bob Santilli waves to kids outside the window and coordinates plans for an end-of-the-week outing.

Not a sound squeaks out of the front room of the second brownstone; a game of pool has started. The shot is played, the ball goes in, then the general cheering. In the back room younger kids sand, paper smooth, the rim of soda bottle trunks to make drinking glasses.

Upstairs others are being tutored in reading and writing. We push the basic skills so the kids will have something to offer. Nineteen-year-old Libby says, *"I learned to read here. Before when I went to look for work, the people asked me to fill out an application. But I couldn't read or write to do it. Now I can. Before at other agencies, if I didn't learn, too bad for me. They didn't care. They had a job. If I did or didn't learn, it was no difference to them."*

Some go on to get a high school equivalency, and some to college. Counselors double as teachers and cheerleaders to keep the kids studying. False starts are as common as weeds. We try to convince the backslider to take another crack, sometimes a dozen times. The reward comes when a kid finds out for himself he can do it, and gets a diploma.

The counselors also try to wedge kids into training programs, but they are chronically overcrowded. We're straight with the kids, no promises if there aren't any jobs. All the while, they are calling around in case one turns up but employers are weary of inner city kids.

Since it first sidewinded its way into popularity, drug abuse has shattered Harlem lives. Y.D.I. recently set up, under Bob Santilli's urging, a drug prevention center, Crossroads House. It differs from Crossroads Center by being federally, not privately, funded.

Joe Gagos runs the program. He dropped out of school in the eighth grade and got into the drug culture. He picked himself up with Christ's help and got his high school equivalency, then went to a community college. The counselors Gagos hired may know the drug scene even better than he does. They're ex-addicts, just released from prison. This gives Crossroads House some workers who have experience. Each counselor's story is poignant, a tale of rising like a phoenix out of the ashes of his past to begin anew. They have the character to get an addict's attention.

Crossroads House tries to direct kids to drug-free programs, to get them to quit "cold turkey." The other way is to go on to methadone. It was developed to inhibit the effects of heroin and to work as a substitution, just as heroin was developed as an antidote for morphine. *"But, says Gagos, "it is fifteen to twenty times harder to kick, and we don't know the long-range effects. We do know that a methadone "high" tapers off with use, and then kids turn to the old stand-by, cheap wine. But methadone and booze don't mix. Kids aren't dying as much from overdoses today. Instead, they get drunk while on methadone and strangle on their own vomit."*

At Crossroads House and Crossroads Center, you see kids coming back year after year. It seems like they're marking time. *"Just by being there, hanging around with the kids,"* says Santilli, *"you get to know them and eventually their problems and try to help. It may take time for some to make a commitment to the Lord. Some never do, but I can't help thinking we offer a solidity that will rub off."*

18 Chapter

Sporadically, I noticed that my left thumb would involuntarily punch an imaginary button. Weeks later I felt the thumb quiver, as if it were carrying an electric current. Then the unwanted movement was an everyday matter. My local doctor sent me to a neurologist, who shook my right hand, then my left. He asked me to play the piano. I plunked out a simple piece with my right hand, but my left hand lost the rhythm. In five minutes, the doctor diagnosed Parkinson's disease.

The doctor reassured me that no one ever died of Parkinson's disease, but there was no known cure, short of a brain operation. The operation had worked in some cases, but there was no guarantee it would in mine. Without the operation, the disease advances slowly, sometimes only over half the body. I did some checking around, admittedly over-the-back-fence research, and heard of one man with Parkinson who had undergone the operation. His surgeon did knock out the disease, but while doing so cut out a little too much of the man's brain. The surgery left him a healthy vegetable. It may have been one case in a billion, but it made an impression.

"There's no way I'm going to have that operation," I told Alice. I settled for the medication the doctor gave me. It didn't do much. The tremor spread.

I had heard talk of a new, so-called wonder drug, L-Dopa. It was being tested at Einstein Medical Center in New York. The only people taking the drug were a part of the center's research program. I applied to be admitted to that group, but they turned me down because the center was only admitting "hardship" cases. Alice answered that I *was* one. One of my daughters had died, the other was in a mental institution, I'd had polio and a few other lesser diseases, and most important, was doing work others counted on.

Alice's letter opened the center's door to me and I was put on L-Dopa. I still live with Parkinson's disease, but it has slowed. It has spread to my whole left hand, and my left leg isn't as strong as it once was, but without the drug, I might be bent double today.

Even with L-Dopa, it got to be a trick to step smoothly onto a platform and to stand for long periods. Then the eastern winters did me in. Those beautiful snow coated Christmas card scenes became treacherous for me. I frequently lost balance and fell on the shimmering streets. My doctor cautioned me that if I broke a bone on the left side of my body during a fall, it might not heal properly since the tremor never stills. The doctor didn't order me out of the snow country, but he did say that if he faced my problems, he would move to a more hospitable climate. A warm climate to me meant home to California.

We decided on San Diego. The trip west of course meant the end of my day-to-day operation of Y.D.I.

146

After fifteen years of total immersion in the work, I didn't want to shut off my involvement with the programs I had watched grow from infancy. However, under the circumstances the best compromise was one of living in the west and commuting once or twice a month to New York. It was a temporary solution at best.

Desirous of working out my own support I went back to my old love of electronics. I opened a consulting business in the computer field, Coast Computer Corporation.

I joined this with a second corporation in 1972 known as Coast Video Corporation, a TV production house for making features, commercials, covering sports events, both in the studio and on location.

Though I was still closely affiliated with Y.D.I. in the east I wanted to use the experience of the past in establishing a western branch, hoping to reach both the affluent and the impoverished.

Gary Templin, a former Camp Champion director, now director of Outward Bound, helped me father Summit Expedition, a gritty mountaineering program as different from Camp Champion as the coasts are from each other.

Most of the activity begins from a base camp in the high Sierras, northern California. Sounds come from rustling trees and rushing stream water; perfume from the vanilla smell of the Jeffery pines. It is beautiful, and isolated.

There's no plush lodge with bed, bath, and kitchen. The kids carry their sleeping bags, their clothes, their food on their backs. They make their own meals from cheese, pilot biscuits, honey, and packets of dehydrated food they revive with water and cook in tin cans over the open camp fires.

There are no hour-by-hour activities at Summit. Kids roll out of bed and run down and back up the

147

trails before breakfast. If that doesn't wake them up, there's always a nearby icy stream. Kids pack up and are off after breakfast to trailblaze a hike or a climb. The kids have the responsibility of taking care of themselves and lending a hand to others.

At Camp Champion, that would have been a disaster, but Summit kids aren't confined to the bell jar life of Harlem. The kids come from everywhere along the strata of society. Some are on scholarships, siphoned from the tuition of those who can afford to pay.

Two people make it work. Director Tim Hansel, a former high school teacher who got his M.A. at Stanford and who has had experience with Young Life and Outward Bound; and Cris Courter who taught high school after graduation from Stanford.

These kids don't need to be taught to read, nor do they carry knives, but that doesn't mean they don't have problems. One boy had to overcome a fear of heights that literally gave him a twitch. A girl was there to touch base with natural elements; she had a series of operations to thwart cancer and was slowed up because her neck muscles close, choking her when she breathes heavily. It happened once in the midst of a climb up a steep rock. She went on the rest of the way, cheering others by her words and acts.

In the mountains, youth, sealed off from routine pressures, are wrapped in a rare salve, unqualified praise. They earn it. The days are not predictable. A climb that looks from the bottom of the mountain like it ought to take four hours may turn out to be an eight-hour push. But you don't find out until you're half way up. A small group Tim Hansel led made the first half of a climb easily one afternoon. The rest wasn't so simple. The lead climbers made progress, but slowly. Three others waited on a ledge smaller than a bed for their turn to climb. Hansel remembers, *"After three or four hours, we finally made our way up to a stopping point and sent another climber on ahead to the top. The kids were still on the ledge and I heard them call. The wind muffled their words, but I was sure they were shouting 'Get us out of here.' That's just what we were working on. It was getting dark and we had a long way up to go. They called again and I heard 'Look at the moonrise.' It was spectacular, and gave us light to climb by."*

"Aren't you proud you did such a good job?" comes the applause for those who climbed up what looked like a sheer rock face in the moonlight. They pulled themselves up by searching out cracks for footholds and little mole hills on the mountains called "chicken heads" to grab. Listening to praise while standing on the top, taking in the luxury of looking back over the hard-won battle, a kid can't help but give thanks and be proud of himself, perhaps for the first time ever.

Jack Miller, a professional climber and teacher observes: *"After being with a hard bunch of climbers trying to do each other in, it's like magic to be with the kids in this atmosphere of positive reinforcement."*

The atmosphere lets kids risk shedding masks and taking a real look at themselves and others. Fireside dialogues probe the heavy issues that weigh them down. At these informal seminars a kid discovers he is not the only one who is lonely sometimes, or afraid. Together they seek better ways of living.

My son Roger was fifteen when he first went to camp. Alice puts it best; *"Roger went up to the mountains a little boy. He came back a man. The mountains' demands, his time alone, searching studies of Scripture, the interrelationships, worked on him to make him find out where he stood before God. I feel he can handle himself physically and spiritually."*

It's a good feeling, knowing your child is capable of taking care of himself. That's the most a parent can ask as children take off to live their own lives.

Our family circle now seems to encompass the whole

nation with Madeline working in a Christian farming group in Mississippi, Dennis completing seminary in California, Steve working as a personnel counselor in New York, and Roger in the air force presently in Illinois.

Mickey Cohen is home again after eleven years in prison. During his time on the inside he got an anonymous blow on the head that fractured his skull. The doctors told him he'd never walk again, but with the aid of therapy treatments and his own fierce determination, Cohen gets around, if a bit stiffly, with a cane.

Cohen's lifestyle has toned down. When we occasionally dine together he still over tips, but nothing like the old days. For one thing, he doesn't worry about dirty money, he has a Master Charge card.

"Things changed over eleven years, like the coming of credit cards," says Cohen. "When I came home, my credit rating in the community was completely wiped out. I had to re-establish myself. A friend of mine, a former lieutenant of police, took me over to open a bank account. He told the accountant to put in for a Master Charge for me. I wasn't even sure that it was at the time. I must have been remembered from other days and I had no trouble! I got a card with credit for a thousand dollars. When the lieutenant called to find out if I'd got the card, he asked what my line of credit was. I told him. 'You dirty gangster,' he said. (I don't mind this talk from a friend of mine.) 'I'm a retired lieutenant, a property owner, a respected citizen, and I only have credit for five hundred.' "And," says Cohen, "I don't even feel good using it. I've got to force myself. It's like stiffing a guy, you know, like not paying up.

"Life is a whole new ball game since I've come home. A lot of other things are different. I don't think you could put together an operation like mine today. So many have passed on, and there've been changes in thinking. They do things with such carelessness, without any forethought about who they connect up with. It used to be a closed, family situation. You had to be tried

and tested before you got close. Now everything's spread out. Not that the old times were perfect, mind you. It was a lot like The Godfather. *There was a lot to that book. Of course, you could write from here to eternity on what they left out."*

That's what Cohen is doing, writing his book. Only this time, he is working on a settlement with the IRS so it can be published and leave him some money to live on.

19

Chapter

As my life got more firmly rooted in the west, I fretted over the fact that I wasn't doing justice to Y.D.I. My commuting cross-country every couple of weeks allowed me just enough time to settle the most pressing issues. I inevitably had to let some things slide for long periods or deal with them over the telephone wires. And the time between visits left an empty gap in leadership.

One answer was to replace myself, which I did with Alec and Rita Rowlands. I met them at a youth rally in Ohio. Alec, who had completed work on his M.A. in urban geography, was minister of youth at St. Clair Avenue Baptist Church. Rita was directing a musical group. She's something to see in action. Her cheerleader looks mask her no-nonsense ability to whip kids into shape and get them to perform. I knew those two would be great for something, but I didn't know what. What I needed at the time was information on how Y.D.I. was doing, so I sent them to New York to report on Y.D.I. programs.

Alec and Rita did an excellent job sorting out Y.D.I.'s strengths and weaknesses and making some recommendations for change. I asked them to stay on. Alec took over the function of executive director and with a maturity far beyond his age, managed Y.D.I.'s city and camp programs skillfully. The Rowlands' real love is music ministry and while in New York they formed a group, with three others called the "Master Design". Even with the Rowlands' help, I couldn't let go of the responsibility of fund-raising.

To strengthen the weak link in Y.D.I., I have carved out a new arrangement to provide stronger leadership for the New York program. There will be a separate director in the east. Alec and Rita Rowlands and the "Master Design" singing group are part of the western branch of Y.D.I.; it will continue to assist Y.D.I. in the east with limited financial support. The present Y.D.I. staff, with the exceptions of the Rowlands, will keep on with their work in New York.

After all the years, I sever my tie with Y.D.I. in New York with a twinge of regret, but with a great sense of pride and satisfaction at our accomplishments to date and confidence in a rich future. And, in that ending, I've found energy for a new beginning. At Y.D.I. in the west we're shifting our focus while continuing our basic theme of help to young people. We're turning our attention to our own troubled backyard and a problem which is larger than that of Hell Gate, runaway teenagers.

We all remember the national horror when the graves, piled high with the bodies of youth, were dug up in Houston, Texas. That incident etched itself onto my psyche and haunted me. I wondered what was happening to the rest of the homeless children. I did research into the problem and found runaways to be a new American phenomenon. They're a group of destitute youngsters from every segment of society, bound together only by their common plight. Their families haven't a clue to their whereabouts and no way to find them.

According to an NBC special, San Diego County is a center for drifting runaways who cluster in the warm climate of the open-armed beach communities. The runaways have no place to go. They seek shelter in cemeteries, laundromats, or linger on the streets. They become targets for dope peddlers and hustlers. Girls are defenseless against sexual assaults. If caught by the authorities, a runaway is treated like a criminal. It is against the law to run away. A child, until he comes of age, is bound to his parents. Generally, the kid gets little sympathy from the public, fed up with too many years of the youth cult. People figure that if the runaways have it tough, they have it coming to them.

According to San Diego County's chief of probation and the heads of juvenile hall and juvenile court the problem is getting worse. There are two homes for runaways in the county. One can handle six kids, the other eight. The police report they have a steady stream of seventy kids and there isn't anywhere else to send them except to detention homes.

Y.D.I. is establishing a place for runaways, Samaritan's Ranch. This is an alternative to jail and detention homes. We have a five-acre miniature of Camp Champion, complete with a lake and twenty adjacent acres for expansion. As we are able to enlarge the number of homes on the ranch, we'll make room for seventy young people, godly foster parents, and staff who will follow the example of Christ's good samaritan. In this spirit we want to provide lodging to youngsters in need, soothe their wounds and nurse them back to physical and spiritual health.

It is my prayer that Samaritan's Ranch will help America's runaways find their way home. The prodigal son in Luke 15 didn't decide to go home until he "came to his senses." I hope the spiritual counsel we bring will return these youngsters to their senses. At the ranch we'll have the opportunity to talk to them and discover why they ran, for running is often the first sign of a family in crisis. We'll try to reunite families that have come unraveled. In some cases where parents don't offer love or care, we'll take over with foster care under the guidance and supervision of the courts.

Y.D.I. will work to make the Samaritan's Ranch a force others will follow, joining our efforts to build facilities and legislation to protect forsaken children now doomed to wander the wastelands.

As when I walked into Harlem, I am still running against the current social concerns. When the act of beginning Samaritan's Ranch seems too large a task for a single person to tackle, I think of Harlem and our faith in action there. I had to confront people, especially church people, with the desperate need for social outreach in the days before civil rights protests and marches. It was a lonely beginning, but people who saw our work there were drawn to extend their hands. And today I'll have to wring out interest for lost lonely kids with long hair and different lifestyles. I have faith in Samaritan's Ranch, for only by being the good samaritan can we live our lives to meet Christ's standards as set forth in the Epistle of James:

> Dear brothers, what's the use of saying that you have faith and are Christians if you aren't proving it by helping others? Will that kind of faith save anyone? If you have a friend who is in need of food and clothing, and you say to him, "Well, good-bye and God bless you; stay warm and eat hearty," and then don't give him clothes or food, what good does that do?

156

So you see, it isn't enough just to have faith. You must also do good to prove that you have it. Faith that doesn't show itself by good works is no faith at all—it is dead and useless (James 2:14-16, Living Bible).

If you are a young person
sensing desperate need,
please let me help you.
Write to me—
 Jim Vaus
 Youth Development, Inc.
 Box 9429
 San Diego, California 92109

Bill Vaus

Jim and Alice Vaus

Roger Vaus

Steve Vaus

Dennis
and
Grace
Vaus